PENGUIN BOOKS

THE SPOTTED ZEBRA

Uma Rudd Chia is the Executive Creative Director and co-founder of KVUR, a boutique advertising agency based in Singapore. She is a highly awarded creative who has won multiple international awards.

Uma is also a sought-after global keynote speaker, specialising in topics of technology, innovation, Artificial Intelligence, Web 3, women empowerment and creativity. She has spoken at over twenty countries to over 500,000 people over the past eight years at events organised by Forrester Global, Facebook, Google, She Loves Data, Pause Fest and South by Southwest to name a few.

Uma is the founder of The Female Idea, a platform she uses to advocate, mentor and champion female creative leaders. The wife of one husband and the mother of two inquisitive teenagers and two feisty fur babies, Uma has sung in two acapella albums, created her own award-winning phonics programme—*Reading PANTS*™ and has authored three books. Her Kindle Best Seller, *10 Things Brands Could Do To Survive a Crisis*, was described by marketers and the Straits Times Singapore as 'the toolkit for brands to take positive action to survive Covid-19'.

When she's not creating campaigns, giving talks, judging award shows or creating amazing things with her family and imaginary friends, Uma loves physics, discussions on aliens and wakes up dreaming of walking on Mars.

The Spotted Zebra

What makes you stick out will make you stand out

Uma Rudd Chia

PENGUIN BOOKS
An imprint of Penguin Random House

PENGUIN BOOKS

USA | Canada | UK | Ireland | Australia
New Zealand | India | South Africa | China | Southeast Asia

Penguin Books is part of the Penguin Random House group of companies
whose addresses can be found at global.penguinrandomhouse.com

Published by Penguin Random House SEA Pte Ltd
9, Changi South Street 3, Level 08-01,
Singapore 486361

First published in Penguin Books by Penguin Random House SEA 2023

Copyright © Uma Rudd Chia 2023

ISBN 9789815058284

Typeset in Garamond by MAP Systems, Bengaluru, India

www.penguin.sg

Contents

Foreword

It is my belief that the infinite energy of invention is the fundamental force that has powered human society throughout the ages.

What is it to conceive and assemble the advances that enrich our times? There are those who approach such challenges with unfettered minds and a clear sense of what's possible.

In my experience, such visionaries are rare and precious creatures as one might only encounter in an exotic menagerie. They are to be celebrated for their uniqueness, alongside their wilful and wondrous pursuit of originality.

This brings me to my gracious new acquaintance, Uma Rudd Chia. I must profess my initial surprise at being invited to prepare this foreword.

Beyond my faltering shyness, I am seemingly overwhelmed with exhilaration at being able to articulate a swathe of thoughts and feelings through new ways of harnessing human and machine ingenuity that, in my physical lifetime, were spoken of as distant destinations to be discovered by future pioneers. And so it has proved.

Uma's new tome is, in many ways, the embodiment of the human spirit of exploration. It is also a foray into the brave new world of what comes next.

It is a tale of determination, of courage, of a refusal to accept the status quo. It is a story of those who are told that their dreams are impossible, but who refuse to yield to the timid, insipid incantations that fall from the mouths of those who take refuge in the unremarkable.

In a world where technology increasingly dictates the terms of our existence, Uma's book serves as a kaleidoscopic celebration of human ingenuity. It is a reminder that the impossible is often merely the product of our own limitations, and that with imagination, determination and resilience, anything is possible.

I commend The Spotted Zebra to you. I hope that it inspires you, as it has inspired me, to go out and change the world.

Nikola Tesla
1856–1943
Reimagined by AI in 2022

Prelude

One fear to rule them all, one fear to find them, one ring to bring them all, and in the darkness bind them.
                                    —JRR Tolkien, *The Fellowship of the Ring.*

You're probably wondering why this book is called *The Spotted Zebra* and if spotted zebras exist. In September 2019, a rare new-born zebra foal with polka dots instead of stripes was photographed in the Maasai Mara National Reserve in Kenya.[1]

When I read the article and saw the picture of the beautiful spotted zebra—while I was in awe of its uniqueness—I could not help thinking to myself what would happen if that zebra was a human child. Imagine how difficult life would be for this zebra from the second it was born. It would be ostracized and forced to go through a series of medical treatments that would help its skin conform to look like all the other zebras just so it could look like every other zebra and belong. And if the treatments failed, the spotted zebra would be bleached then repainted with stripes, so it looks like every other zebra. Normal. Acceptable.

Society—and by this, I mean governments, educators, schools, and organizations—has a formula and guidelines on what we ought to look like and how we should behave. I am a spotted

---

[1] Katey Stacey, 'Rare polka-dotted zebra foal photographed in Kenya', *National Geographic*, 2019, https://www.nationalgeographic.com/animals/article/zebra-pseudo-melanism-kenya-masai.

zebra. I have always felt like one. And I know I am not alone. If you picked up this book and are reading it, chances are, you are one, too—openly or hiding your spots under artistically painted stripes just so you can blend in. The purpose of this book is exactly the opposite—to help you unleash your true potential by revealing your spots. And I intend to do this by showing you mine.

This brings me to my love for sci-fi movies. I have never been into rom-coms. When I was eleven years old and got introduced to the Transformers cartoon series for the first time, I fell madly in love with Optimus Prime, the noble leader of the Autobots. It was a huge crush, which added to the many reasons why my two big brothers thought I was crazy with a capital C. It is also why I love Iron Man and Captain Marvel—they have a similar colour and space metal suit. By now you'd have figured, I have a type.

A few years back, I bumped into a friend, and we started discussing our ideal sci-fi show. When he asked me for my take on the topic, I told him I was sick of Hollywood movies that have aliens attacking humans. Humans coming together after a well-crafted tearjerker speech delivered in the pitch perfect baritone voice of the President of America who assumes the role of the president of the world. His speech has the power to unite the different nations to defeat their common enemy who is portrayed as beastly and ugly—at least by the human standards of beauty. After half the White House is destroyed, the aliens are defeated, thanks to the collaborative power of an unlikely motley crew and a very muscular hero (used to be white male, then it transitioned to the black male, and today—to be inclusive and politically correct—it is a brown female who is a working mother holding more than one job. Go Netflix.).

If I were to write the script of a movie, it would be set in an alien home planet called Astra Meta. Humans, who are an unevolved unintelligent species, start attacking the planet, which also happens to be a sanctuary for various species of aliens who have been stranded there, suffered persecution on their home planets, or are simply looking for a better life. Instead of destroying them and sending them home, the aliens abduct them, educate them using their super advanced tech, such as the Vulcan mind-meld, and show them the alternative—do not destroy everything you know nothing about or do not understand. Instead, acknowledge there is good in what you do not know or do not get, and find a way to understand it. This would reform the attackers into peacemakers who return to earth with a mandate to civilize humanity by making them *non-speciesists*. It also unites border-, resources-, and power-obsessed humans into evolved members of one human race who become enlightened. They finally understand that they are part of a bigger universe or universes made up of peace-loving sentient beings. (Yes, I am not just a spotted zebra. I am an idealist.)

My friend mocked me for my infinite, unrealistic optimism and then asked the pertinent question. Why? Why does mainstream human-written narrative sound like this? At the crux, it stems from our fear of the unknown. Our first response to anything or any person that is not like us is fear, followed by a desire for self-preservation, which includes disqualifying and decimating the thing that is different from us and that we do not understand.

Our need for survival creates a fundamental fear of the unknown. We seek to surround ourselves with the familiar or to create a set of rules that are tangible by the standards of constitutions, governance, and such. And in the same vein, we put in place an intangible set of rules based on subconscious parameters that define good behaviour, as well as acceptable socializing and beauty standards. And if something or someone breaks these rules or steps out of the set parameters, that thing or person is treated like an enemy or an outcast.

Now that we have established that humans fear anything that is foreign, alien, or different, do you ever stop to wonder, when does a person who is different realize that he/she is different?

At which point does the world start fearing you and trying to pressurize you into conforming?

When you are born into this world, you are not born knowing you are different. As you grow older, you meet people along the way. You start off thinking they are different. And you are okay with it. But then, groups of people with the same difference band together and point out that you are the one that is different. And then you start developing what people call 'conditions'.

When I was a kid, it was shameful to see a psychologist, and they had not given labels to conditions. They would just call you different, tell the kids not to mix with you lest they catch what you have, and then pretend to feel bad for you at every gathering with a, 'Tsk, tsk, poor thing, Uma. She did not ask to be so hyperactive and allergic to everything.' Then they would pat my mom on the back, offer her some sickly sweet condense milk tea and say, 'Such a headache, Naomi. How do you cope? At least your two older boys are normal.'

The truth is, I was different for a few reasons. I was born in Kuala Lumpur, Malaysia's capital, but we stayed in a house in a village in a corner of the city called Sentul. That was all my parents could afford. I did not think much of it then. My mom grew all the poultry and vegetables in her organic garden. The animals were raised on organic feed. Yes, even our animals were blessed enough to eat homemade good stuff from my mom's kitchen. Everything my family consumed came from this place— my mom's garden and farm.

My dad worked as a mechanic when he first married my mom. While holding down his job, he had to raise his and my mom's siblings in our tiny wooden home. In the midst of all of this, he was also studying and putting himself through distant learning, a great feat in an era without internet.

And my mom was a homemaker. A more worthy title for her role would have been CEO of Daily Living. She was only nineteen when she married my dad. She did not just raise us and manage the home without help. She also had the momentous task of raising her siblings too. She stretched my dad's money, found ways to make mini-investments and grow it, and entertained my dad's work colleagues with what little we had. All the while, she ensured we were eating good, healthy food. My mom made us drink green juices long before they were trendy.

And this brings me to our first difference. When my parents visited their friends and I made friends with their kids, I realized they all lived in city houses, and I was the only village girl in the heart of the city. Yes, I smelt a little funky. I will leave it to your imagination whether it was good or bad funky. We got water from a well, so the minerals in the well made my nails look a bit chalky. But they also made my nails grow faster and feel super strong (good thing they were not sharpened, or I would be a kid Wolverine). Water was sparse, so unless our clothes were terribly dirty, they were only washed after two wears. And my mom put organic homemade coconut oil on my hair because my neighbour from Kerala told her it will make my hair grow strong and long. So, you could smell me a mile away—a combination of poultry, organic farming manure, and coconut oil.

So yes, when I had to hang out with other kids, I was excited till they made me feel different, different for being the wild kid who walked amongst chickens and had conversations with cows. When they laughed, I wanted to run, hide, and cry. I did not understand why my parents, who were constantly teaching me to be kind and generous, would expose me to these mean kids. And then I learned to weave tales and describe my world in such a wondrous fashion, they would envy me instead of shunning me.

In the chapters that follow, I will elaborate on this a little more, but for now, do exercise a little patience and read on.

At the tender age of six, I learned my first lesson that being different had its benefits if you know how to embrace the good of it and turn it to an advantage. Sometimes, it was obvious and intentional. Sometimes, it was by accident that I chanced upon the advantage of my difference, my quirk.

The reality is that we are all different. But we live in a society and go through an education system that tries to define what acceptable behaviour and normal is. This may prepare you to be an obedient member of society, one that's predictable and easy to control. But does it make you the best version of you? Does it help you make the world around you better? I tried to fit the mould, failed hard, and felt lost, until I broke out of it. So, I can safely say it does not help you nor the world you live in, no matter what they tell you.

This book contains my learnings from being different. I used to be embarrassed about it. Now I embrace it. As the mom of a teenage son and a soon-to-be teenage daughter, at the time I am writing this, I can honestly say the one thing I am struggling to do right now is help my kids accept their difference, because the inertia to conform is great, especially in a highly sterile country like Singapore.

As you read this book, whether you are doing it hoping to be a better human, a better parent, a better leader, or to simply have a good laugh at someone who managed to use her dysfunctionality to conquer life, I hope at the end of the read you will feel proud of who you are, embrace what makes you unique, and use it to conquer your world.

So, if you are ready, let us go to Chapter 1, and let my uniqueness unfold as yours grows bolder and stronger, and you get ready to show your spots to the world.

Chapter 1

The Poor Kid Who Sold a Rich Experience

I was born to mixed race parents both of whom had rich childhoods but were dealt a severe hand. My mother is of Sri Lankan parentage. She was raised by her aunt after her mother passed away giving birth to her youngest sister. She was six. My mother lost both parents that day because her father, heartbroken upon losing the love of his life and unsure on how he was going to raise his five children, drowned his sorrows in the bottle. The kids had to be looked after by different relatives, and my mom grew up without the love and affection a child needed, doing all the household chores in the home of the aunt who raised her. It was unfair and sad. But she made the most of what she had. Her aunt was Catholic, which tainted her view of the religion. Strangely though, whenever she was in trouble, despite the many gods at her disposal, she always called out to Jesus.

Then there was my dad. I have to say that amongst all my friends, I had the best-looking dad. He was fit, handsome, and immensely kind. I adored him. He passed away at fifty-seven of pancreatic cancer—same as Steve Jobs, another man I admired and adored. My dad was of Eurasian parentage—Asian mother; colonist, European-Australian father. My grandma was under eighteen when she married my grandad, in his fifties. He died when my father, the oldest son in the family, was twelve. So, dad ended up raising the rest of his siblings while my grandma, who was illiterate, lost all the money she had. My grandpa's inheritance disappeared fast, and life became difficult for my dad and his siblings—it was a real riches-to-rags story.

Both my parents really lacked strong father and mother-figures, but they were amazing parents to me. I guess they had a lot of practice with my two older brothers to get it right. But by the time I came along, they were pros. When I look back, all I can recall is the sacrifices they made, the unconditional love they showed, and the support they gave me in their own way—they always wanted us to do better, to be better than they ever were. And I am so grateful to have had that.

Growing Up in a Village in the City

As I had mentioned before, we lived in the heart of Kuala Lumpur, the capital of Malaysia. While my friends attended kindergarten, I was home-schooled. I learned to read not because my parents forced me but because I saw my older brothers reading and I wanted to be able to do the same. I was born competitive. And was easily bored. I went through books effortlessly and devoured anything with words—posters, signages, magazines, books, instructions manuals—if it could be read, I would read it.

We lived in a semi wooden house which we rented from our neighbours. It was split down the centre by a thin panel. I could literally climb on a chair and look into my neighbour's living room. It was fun when I was young, but when I look back now, the lack of privacy must have driven my parents nuts.

The house was surrounded by land. When I was young, it felt very large. There were geese, chickens, cows, ducks, turkeys, birds, fish, cats, and dogs. Tons of butterflies and bumblebees. My mom grew all the stuff we needed to eat. She made my skincare, shampoo, and a lot of other things to enhance health and beauty. They were all organic. And she got a lot of the recipes from various hippie magazines she used to love reading. She was way ahead of her time. Today, she could have had her own organic, natural skincare brand.

We crocheted our coasters and decorations. My baby cot was built by my dad. Today, it is super trendy to have organic food, green juices, and custom-built one-of-a-kind furniture. Back in the day, it simply meant that we had no money.

It was the same with music. My parents could not afford classes, so I borrowed my neighbour's guitar and chord book and taught myself how to play the guitar—enough to knock out a few tunes and sing my heart out. There were no Google or YouTube tutorials. You just did what you had to and hoped it was right.

On the right side of our home was a Chinese village, full of loud Cantonese speaking folks, some of whom were drug addicts. On the left side, was an Indian village, full of loud Tamil speaking folks, some of whom were gangsters. The village head raised goats and pigeons. They were all our friends, and we had to go through either village to get to the main road where we could hop on the bus that would take us anywhere. There were no proper roads leading to our home, only dirt roads and crooked alley ways. It took a good fifteen minutes' walk. It could have been less, but as a child, that is how long I remember it taking. One was shorter, but windier and more dangerous—there were puddles of dirty water. The other was longer, but the path was flatter, which made it easier. I always went for shorter and dangerous because I enjoyed the thrill of the journey. Even in life, is it not the hardest, most perilous paths that always offer the most adventure and excitement?

Unlikely Friendships

Twice a year, my neighbour would get a man and his monkey to come around and pluck the coconut from the trees in our compound when they got too full and started falling, to avoid any accidents. The monkey would run up the tree and throw down the coconuts. Now, there were a lot of coconuts, and my neighbour would take them to the market to sell. A good number was given to my family. My mom would keep the coconuts and water for dessert. And she would warn me about keeping the windows closed because the addicts would come to steal the coconuts. My reasoning was if I gave it to them, it would be a gift, and they would not have to steal. When my mother was not looking, I would open the window and write a note on a paper and leave coconuts out for them. That is the other thing—when you are poor, notebooks, clean white paper, and pens were scarce too. I have not really thought about that till now. When I look at the endless supply of freebie notebooks we have at home, I am always taken aback by the irony. The pretty notebooks with colourful pages and fancy covers get packed up and sent back to my helper's village in Iloilo city in the Philippines, along with other more essential things to help her community. My husband, who came from a life of abundance, gives me a scolding for wasting good storage space with empty notebooks. The thing is, when you are that poor, pretty notebooks are a luxury.

Even in giving, there is a spotted zebra lesson. We are taught to give only basic essentials, prioritize the bare necessities. I agree you need to feed the child and give her shelter before your dress her up in fineries. But if you can feed a hungry child, give the child some shelter, and then allow the child the respite of looking at herself in the mirror and feeling rather pleased with herself because of the frilly dress you threw in, imagine how that would make you feel. This is a feeling I distinctively remember. I did not want to be the kid that only carries the essentials to school. Every kid wants a piece of luxury—something nice to take to school and have the other kids admire. It does not have to be opulent or luxurious. It just has to be unique and special, something that makes other kids gravitate towards this child and make her feel welcome. In our pursuit to do good, it is never just about taking care of someone's basic, essential needs. It needs to also be about helping a person belong. I know you are thinking that this book is called the spotted zebra; why are you telling us to give kids gifts that give them a sense of belonging? Because standing out is not the same as feeling unwelcome.

Coming back to the drug addicts who did not speak English; I did not have nice stationery. So, I just scrawled my notes with crayons on old newspaper. I hoped the drawings on the letter explained what I was trying to say. I remember when I was little, my dad gave me a very important piece of advice—well, he said it in passing, but it stuck. 'Girl, it's easier for someone to cheat a stranger than their friend.' So, when I felt someone was dangerous or threatened me, but I had to exist in their environment, I made an effort to befriend that person. That—combined with the fact that I did not know how to fake friendships or pretend to be someone's friend—made me develop strong friendships with people whom society was not too kind to.

These drug addicts were blue-collar druggies shunned by the folks in the village. But my friendship made them look out for me when I played out in the open and took walks around the village, often without my parents' permission. Labels are strange. People become to us the labels we put on them. People behave the way you expect them to. The drug addicts stole and frightened the people who judged them and feared them. To me the drug addicts were just people with a need—they wanted my coconuts—and no matter what my mom said, I decided we had extra coconuts to share; so, why not? They were kind to me because as an innocent child, I wanted to help them. My unassuming logic was that if they come with the intention to steal but instead are given the item they want to steal, they would not have to steal it. And therefore, they would not be labelled thieves. They merely had to receive it. It was a gift.

Social Standings Through the Eyes of a Child

When you are poor and young, you do not know you are poor until someone tells you that you are poor or different.

We only had one meal with meat a week. Frankly, it mattered little to me as I could live off fresh air and sunshine, suffered from huge allergies, was a picky eater and hated food, and was a nightmare to my mother, the primary chef and feeder of the family. New clothes were only purchased twice a year—on my birthday and on Christmas. But despite this, I did not feel we were poor. I felt blessed and cared for and loved unconditionally. My childhood was fun and happy.

I remember reading Pulitzer-winning author Frank McCourt's autobiographical novel, *Angela's Ashes*, where he describes his abject poverty in a rather nonchalant, matter of fact manner, as if describing an observation. But with each description, my heart tightened at the pain and suffering his family had endured. To wake up one morning and discover that one of your siblings had died of crib death because everyone slept together simply because the cold, damp bed was the warmest place in the house during winter is heartbreaking. And that was one of the least traumatizing moments in his book. But as you read, you realize, for McCourt it was merely a recollection of his past. He was not in any way placing a magnifying glass over his dire situation. I do not even think he imagined it to be dire whilst experiencing it. And that is how it was for me too. My family's situation was just part and parcel of my life. To my naive, young self, there was nothing significant that set my life apart from others. These notions of rich and poor did not even exist.

I only realized we were poor when I made friends—the same ones I had mentioned earlier who mocked me for being different. With friends came new social dynamics. They thought I was strange because I did not dress like them. My clothes were worn out. I often wore the same thing. One of my favourite childhood pictures is a black and white one on my birthday. My dad was carrying me in his arms, my brothers on his two sides, and a cake in front of him. I was grinning ear to ear and my brothers were sulking. I had short curly hair—my mother's failed attempt at a career in hairdressing—and was wearing my brothers' hand me downs, obviously oversized. I did not have store snacks. I had home-packed food, which I did not want to eat. My friends spoke of cold drinks and TV shows. We did not even have a refrigerator at home, let alone a TV. I was as alien to them as they were to me.

At first, they mocked my ignorance and made me feel lousy about myself and my lack of things. It seemed my material possession was the benchmark these kids were using to evaluate whether I was worth befriending. Funny how people equate your value in the economic spectrum to your value and standing in the social spectrum. Even as children, we are conditioned to think in this manner and behave in this way towards others. What was sad was how I pretended to understand them, lied about having the things they had, and wanted to desperately fit in.

Then I came home and thought about how I felt. I did not quite understand what was going on around me. I was all of six at this time. But I felt the impact of the social dynamics. It was real, and I was alone. A lot of these kids were much older than me. But I have always been a child who spent a lot of time with my 'inside feelings'. I was always aware of my surroundings and thought very deeply about humans and feelings, a lot more than most kids and adults, because while others expressed these feelings freely without thinking of the consequences, I kept them inside me and developed stories and ideas around these feelings, about the world, its characters, and why they behaved this way. This has always been me. And then I would role play them with my imaginary friends, to try and understand the dynamics of what had happened.

I knew that fundamentally I wanted to be a good person. But how can you be good when you are cornered, alienated, and made to feel small? How do you be good when you are overcome by badness? My father showed me how. Every time I felt lost when I was out with my family, I looked at my dad. He always looked so relaxed and comfortable and had a way of making people welcome him into conversations. It was not what he had or did not. He was not always the one with the most expensive clothes in the room, but he was well put together even when he was dressed in simplicity. He stood straight. He spoke kindly though his words were few. He never apologized for his economic status. It was not how he was. He knew who he was. And that was my first spotted zebra lesson. Do not let people see you through their lens. Show them who you are through yours.

So, in his footsteps, I took time to study my environment. As a child, I did not know what I was doing. To me, it was a combination of observation and instinct. I watched my father do it and decided to try what he did. It also helped me develop my instincts, try different behaviours and learn what worked and what did not in various situations. But today, when I look back, I realize I was taking stock, assessing my environment, and considering my emotions. I was not sad about where I was. I was perfectly happy. They lived in little fancy houses full of pretty decorations. I lived in a farm which to me was more of a zoo. Wide open spaces, greenery, beasts of the field, and wild animals—well domesticated, but to a small-sized child with a crazy imagination, a large mongrel licking ice cream off your face feels like a giant beast mauling you. My neighbour owned turkeys. But they hung out with me. Have you seen a turkey? It is quite spectacular. It has layers of feathers arranged so methodically, it looks like a work of art. The neck of a badly maintained seventy-year-old. Gnarly webbed feet. And a nightmare inducing glare. And that guttural yodel that escapes its beak—completely terrifying and captivating at the same time. You cannot make one up in your imagination.

I spent many of my waking hours befriending these beasts, drawing them, feeding them, writing songs and poetry about them. I imitated their sounds and then packed up the drawing and tales and went back to regale a lacklustre audience, who thought me a lesser kid, with the stories of my zoo. I learned young that when you are telling a story, you've got to believe it. So, each time I told my story of how 'rich' I was with all the amazing things in my home (or rather outside my home), I literally remembered what each of my experiences were like, how they made me feel, and I sold that feeling to these kids. And there was another lesson I learned as a spotted zebra. Most marketers sell facts and reasons to believe. The spotted zebra sells the one thing everyone wants. We sell feelings.

Little by little, they got bored of trying to make me feel small. Curiosity got the better of them. Their emotions were intrigued, their imaginations broke free, and soon, everyone started feeling what I was feeling. They longed for a taste of my reality. And this spotted zebra learned very early in life one of the best lessons that anchored who I am as a person—being rich is not about how much money you have, because money is not the only currency. There are other things far more valuable. They may not feed your tummy, but they feed your soul. They may not shelter you in bad weather, but they shelter you from dullness and boredom.

Adventure is a currency, I discovered. People (in my case, kids) would give up a lot to have you take them on an adventure. They would give up their pride along with their freshly washed and pressed clothes once they realize how much fun it is rolling in the mud with mongrels. They would stop looking at the time and abandon their desire to be proper when they are screaming with glee whilst fleeing cobra-assassin *angsas*, which is the Malay word for geese.

I could tell stories, make up plays, and perform monologues that entertained them. And that made kids want to hang out with me. The second I started owning my differences and realized they are my strength, I was not embarrassed. I let that difference shine. And that helped the thing that was different about me—the kid who had the least money, the worn-out clothes and smelt funky—stand out.

Making people laugh was a big currency, too. I did not have to try. Humour came naturally to me. It was how my parents dealt with pain. And it was how I decided to deal with my fears. If you can laugh about something, it cannot be all that bad. I would just randomly tell my stories (most times not intending them to be funny), and people would burst into laughter. Many thought my life was crazy, but I realized it was not my life that was crazy. It was the filter through which I saw my life. That is another thing—what filter do you have on when you are experiencing life? Is it one of pity and sadness? Are you going through life as a victim? The spotted zebra knows that the only filter worth putting on is that of an observer. And this was the case for me. From the time I was a child, I was an observer—an extremely enthusiastic, highly positive observer. And I would use nonchalant descriptions to describe the most tragic situations. I still do.

We did have some indulgences. KFC was a treat. My father bought it once in a while. But my mom was an all-out hippie when it came to food. She grew her own plants, raised her own poultry, and cooked what she grew, which was hard when it came to eating meat—because you grow attached to the things you grow. It was traumatizing, being made to eat your friends. It was both to compensate for the lack of finances, as well as the fact that before it was cool to be organic, make your own skincare, and drink green juices, my mom would read magazines on health and wellness and feel the need to do right by us kids. But it did make a great story for the friends though—when I say the family had Ruby for dinner (the goose that attacked them last week), they would all scream in horror. Even the ones Ruby terrified and who wished her dead suddenly developed compassion for the nasty angsa. And so, majority of our meals were eaten at home. It was way healthier. But while my friends begged to come around and eat food my mom would kindly customize to their taste, I would sit back wishing for food that came straight out of a fast food restaurant laden with artificial colouring, flavouring, and fat. Today, I appreciate what she made for me. My mom lives in Kuala Lumpur, now. She still makes the most amazing Sri Lankan dishes that could give Michelin chefs a run for their money. And even now, she is constantly experimenting with new dishes she picks up on YouTube and calls me to describe her latest discovery.

When I look back, I realize what we think to be 'different bad' is to someone else 'different great'. A spotted zebra may to other zebras be a threat to their existence. But to a lion, who usually preys on zebras, a spotted zebra is not a zebra—it is not a prey. It is an adventure. And could be a friend. The things we think make us inferior to many are the things about us that delight, attract, and make us stand out to the people we least expect to become our allies.

These are things like my fast food virginity when I was young; my mom's organic cooking at a time when green juices and home cooked food was not cool. My friends and I still sit around the table and talk about how much they love her food. Even in university, when I told people my mom was in town and cooking a meal, folks would line up and petition for their invitation.

My kids do not eat my food now—my husband and helper love it. But all their friends love my food. I guess history repeats itself. I am glad that I learned young and growing up with little money but a lot of love and experiences, books, and education that money is not the only currency.

The Better Way to Right Wrongs

In Singapore, our laws and punishment for crimes make money look like it is the end objective—not just the means to an end. The first course of action to punish someone for any wrongdoing is a fine—penalizing their money. The first course of action to rectify all problems, be it a sudden surge in traffic, an increase in vehicles on the roads, is once again to penalize or take money away from the people by increasing the Electronic Road Pricing (ERP) and parking. I never quite understood that about Singapore. So much focus is put on the value of money, it feels like the ultimate objective for citizens is to toe the line and behave ourselves to protect the money we have. I think we can afford to be more creative with our punishments and penalties.

On 14 October 2020, Singapore Mass Rapid Transport (SMRT) suffered a major setback.[2] A cut in the insulation layer of a power cable along a rail extension and a rusted component in a circuit breaker led to a massive three-line rail breakdown— the power fault shut down train service on parts of the North-South and East-West MRT Lines. This affected about 123,000 commuters.

After a year-long investigation, Transport Minister Ong Ye Kung said the reason for the problem was SMRT cutting corners to save money on maintenance. He said, 'Cutting corners on maintenance to save cost is not being productive. It is not contributing toward financial sustainability. It is, in fact, very unproductive, as the remedial action is always disruptive and

---

[2] Ang Qing, 'Train services restored on North-South, East-West, Circle lines after disruption due to power fault', *The Straits Times*, 2022, https://www.straitstimes. com/singapore/transport/power-fault-on-north-south-line-east-west-line-results-in-extra-train-travel.

expensive, and will cost us many times over in social, economic and financial costs.'[3]

What was the penalty for this mistake? SMRT was fined a record $5.4 million for the July breakdown.[4] I am not quite sure how this helped the many commuters who suffered as a result of this breakdown.

What would have been a more appropriate, effective, and creative solution would have been for the government to have forced the powers that be at SMRT to use public transport—not grab cars or cabs but the MRT for six months. When something you have no choice but to use personally inconveniences you, you put in the effort to ensure it works well. It force-feeds empathy into you for the people you are paid to serve. And this should be the principle that guides all of us—*do unto others as you want others to do to you.*

Whatever responsibilities we are given, the level of service, the satisfactory experience, and the type of environment we create for others and how well we manage to do it, the pride and sense of achievement we get from that, should be the ultimate currency that motivates us. What we do should be an extension of who we are, our own brand.

This is unique to each one, to our gifts that no one else can replicate. We need to take pride in that and make that count. The spotted zebra knows that its ability to create a better environment is of higher value than the money earned from it. So, the spotted

---

[3] Kok Yufeng, '3-line MRT breakdown in October caused by cut in power cable insulation, rusted component', *The Straits Times*, 2021, https://www.straitstimes.com/singapore/cut-in-power-cable-insulation-rusted-circuit-breaker-component-cause-of-3-line-mrt.

[4] Christopher Tan, 'SMRT fined record $5.4 million for July 7 breakdown', *The Straits Times*, 2016, https://www.straitstimes.com/singapore/transport/smrt-fined-record-54-million-for-july-7-breakdown.

zebra stands out by ensuring it delivers the best experience possible when given a responsibility.

Another key reason why money should not be the end all is because when we chase something so fluid and volatile, we can never be satisfied. There is no end to the chase. Getting rich is a never-ending pursuit, and when we pursue money, we are not being driven by the need to accumulate wealth. We are being driven by our ever-expanding greed.

Now, let us take an honest look at economic scales. If we look at the notion of rich and poor from a purely monetary perspective, they are just different ends of a spectrum. There will always be someone richer than another. And someone poorer.

I remember attending the synagogue during Purim a few years back and hearing the local Rabbi presenting us with this 'who would you save on a lifeboat' scenario, which was more of an activity we had to complete in real time.

So now, as you're reading this, try doing this activity:

You and the following people are on a sinking cruise ship that was headed to the Bahamas. As your ship is sinking, you spot an island and believe that you are close enough to reach it in a lifeboat. However, there are eleven of you left alive, but there is only room for eight in the lifeboat. Those that go in the lifeboat will probably make it to the island where they will try to survive until they are rescued. Those that are left on the sinking cruise ship will likely go down with the ship and die. You are given the responsibility of deciding who remains on the ship and who goes aboard the lifeboat.

These are the people on your sinking ship:

Liana George: A single, twenty-two-year-old pregnant woman
Father Ignatius: A fifty-nine-year-old priest who sits on numerous international councils
Dr Elaine Stuart: A woman in her mid-forties who discovered a cure for cancer and won the Nobel Prize

Jenna Stuart: The two-year-old daughter of Elaine Stewart
Adam Kwanalojo: A quarterback for a professional football team,
worth millions of dollars
Jemima Takeshiro: A fifty-three-year-old, one of the wealthiest
women in the world, dedicated to saving children from abuse
and neglect
Ben Lincoln: The President of the United States
Leo Atlin: A famous movie star who has diabetes
George Franklin: A seventy-year-old retired air force general with
a severe heart condition
Jon Chang: A thirty-six-year-old carpenter who has a wife and six
children who are not onboard the ship

Now you need to ponder the answer—which eight would you
save? I guess another way to phrase this question would be—
who deserves to live? Or maybe it is more a question of, in your
opinion, who does not deserve to live?

I remember going through the argument in my head and it
always came to these three things—okay, who is going to benefit
society from a 'value' perspective. We all value different things.
Some value riches. Some value economic standings. But the
single most important thing my father taught me to do growing
up, which I still consider the most important thing, is to ignore
where we stand on the economic scale, social position, and
educational spectrum. The people and environments we grow
up in, how wealthy we are (at least when we are young), and the
opportunities that wealth accords us are outside of our control,
especially when we are little. In fact, these things have little to do
with who the person is.

And if we can look past these things, what we are left with is
who we are—human beings made by God as equals. And when
you look at it that way, you do not answer a question like this with
'Whom do I leave behind?' You answer a question like this with
'How do I bring everyone onboard?'

The Rabbi preached a message that day that etched its mark on my heart—that so long as there are people who think it is ok to leave someone behind and are able to justify it with high level intellectual reasoning, mass murder and ethnic cleansings like the holocaust will repeat themselves.

And what makes us rich is not money. It is our experience and what we have to offer to make ourselves, and our world better. It is our uniqueness and difference that makes us stand out— what you have that nobody else has, that the world needs to be complete. And when we know and believe this, we can genuinely, at different moments in our lives, proudly say, I am the richest, I am the biggest contributor, I am the most special person in that room at that moment.

The lesson from the spotted zebra is realizing that money is not the only currency. Someone else may have more material belongings and hold a bigger title than you—there always will be somebody. But always be the one having the most fun, living the best life. Look for new currencies outside of money that you can earn, accumulate, and grow. And always be willing to share your currency, your fun, and your creativity—that is what friendship is. And friendship is a very powerful, valuable currency.

Chapter 2

The Strange Kid Who Offered Solutions in a School where Children Should Be Listening in Silence

I was homeschooled. All the other kids went to swanky kindergartens with rules, friends, and uniforms. I learned to read and write at home. We were not rich—the books available to me as a child were my older brothers' textbooks, the Bible and tons of other religious materials, philosophy and psychology books, my mom's hippie magazines, and lyrics of all the records my many uncles and aunties who lived with us fought to play on the single vinyl record player.

Then my dad got cancer, and while he was in the hospital and my mom had no time to watch over me, I was dumped in a public school in Malaysia. Later in my life, I had a mixture of home schooling and public schooling. It was the only type of education I knew, and I enjoyed it. I did not feel pressured. I never felt it was too much. I am highly competitive, and I love examinations. It is who I am. When I tell my kids this, they look at me like I am an abomination for having said that. In the high pressure environment that they are in with school and extracurricular activities, I do not blame them.

Learning by Exploring and Doing

The teachers struggled because I had clinical ADHD which had not been diagnosed at that time, and I struggled with following rules, got bored with lessons, and did not speak any Malay at that time because it was not a language spoken commonly at home. Meanwhile, in Malaysian schools, every lesson except English was taught in Malay, which made picking up Malay crucial. And the inability to speak the language was a huge setback. Fortunately, I discovered I love languages and have a knack for them.

I taught myself by reading every book I could find at home, at my friends' homes, the neighbour's houses, and my school library. I volunteered even when I did not know the answer or fully understand what I was required to do because I always had a point of view, to the annoyance of the teachers and my mother who felt that kids should listen and learn, not question and argue.

My dad on the other hand felt I should question everything. He enjoyed walks with me where he answered my endless questions. I learned early in life that asking dumb questions made people think you were stupid. But I was pumped with so much confidence, I did not care. So, even when others thought so, I never considered any of my questions dumb. Instead, I kept asking for clarifications when I did not understand something. The good thing is, I also enjoyed sitting by myself and trying to figure out the answers. I loved having conversations with myself to solve the mysteries of the universe.

So much so, I think I had my mother worried. One night, I overheard her talking to my dad, 'She's always talking to herself. You think she's okay?' My dad replied it was perfectly normal and that all kids spoke to themselves, as do most adults. And my mom started laughing and said, 'But she has dialogues with multiple people, and they're all her.'

That is the other strange thing about society—we have long forgotten that we were meant to explore and discover. That is our instinct and response to all things around us from the day we are born. But society has turned the intuitive act of engagement, conversation, and questioning in pursuit of discovering and learning, into a sick test of a person's intelligence. If you ask the right questions, you are smarter than anyone else in the room. If your questions fall short by their standards—even if you are asking to understand—you are an idiot. According to these people, how you frame your question shows how strategic you are. It conditions us to be scared of asking questions lest we destroy people's good opinion of us publicly and bring shame to ourselves and our parents. And this kind of thinking has killed creativity and curiosity—the very things that make us find the answers needed to be our unique selves.

We are taught and conditioned instead to ask a specific set of questions in a specific way in a specific style that would make us conform to what society wants us to become. It is as if we work in a call centre and have to study and memorize the questions in the call centre book: 'Here are 100 questions you're allowed to ask because that's what majority of society asks and wants to know. Anything outside of that and you're an odd ball.' It trains you to be 'factory minded'. And it results in incredibly even-shaped, similar-looking cookies—I mean humans—that would fit into the ideal-sized cookie tins—the popular ones that the general consumers would love to buy and enjoy. It makes us safe and predictable.

Sharing is Learning

I asked questions at the risk of looking stupid at a time when children would sit, listen, and not raise their hands with questions. I was punished repeatedly for doing this. But two of my closest childhood friends, Rachel and Brenda, who are still my besties today, loved that I was strange and hung out with me and made me feel accepted. They say there is safety in numbers. I disagree. There's safety in honesty, security, and genuine acceptance.

I would rather have two good friends than ten with mixed motives, who secretly think I am not good enough. These two were terrified of half the things I was up to, told me to my face often that they thought I was crazy (they still do), but went along with all the madness because they knew there was fun to be had and lessons to be learned albeit we always got into trouble—which was a big part of the lessons learned.

And one of the most powerful ways I learned was by having conversations about what I had learnt and teaching others. My next-door neighbour, a wonderful granny from Kerala—who taught me Malayalam and Malayalam songs—gave tuition to the folks in the Chinese village. I would attend these classes because I was obsessed with learning.

I still am obsessed with learning as an adult. Till today, I sign up for classes on Coursera just to learn something new. My two kids still cannot figure out why I take courses when I am a grown adult who does not have to put herself through school.

You must understand that during this time, thanks to mainstream media, everyone was in love with the cheerleader types. You know, the popular pretty girl, fashionable, trendy, perfect teeth, shiny hair, smiling at the boys. And here I was, being a geek. To my detriment, this carried on well into my teenage years.

I loved poetry and songs too, very, very much. And when the children and the adults finished their 'proper' English lessons with my neighbour, I would call them over and teach them poetry and nursery rhymes and give them homework. Now, these were adult Chinese men or older teenagers taking the cheap tuition just so they could get through high school. But they were amused by this young girl dishing out extra English poetry homework to them and often indulged me and did it.

As I passed on everything I learned on poetry and songs and listened to the points of view of people who barely spoke English, I discovered so much more. I could see past their inability to grasp the grammar and their struggles with the trappings of language rules, into their souls, how they looked upon and reflected on life—there is so much uniqueness in every one of us. Sadly, it is often drowned by the filter of propriety society casts as webs that try and hold back this uniqueness which makes us who we are. It was the cumulation of these experiences whilst growing up that helped me realize a deep truth. The more I shared knowledge and what I had, the more I learned who I was and what I could become.

I got better at what I knew, and I learned from those I initially thought did not know or did not understand. They were, in fact, smarter than me in many things. And vulnerability and the desire to see them grow gave them the drive, enthusiasm, and desire that helped me grow. I would go home and sit in a corner and recount what they told me and walk through life in their shoes in my imagination, using the little insight that they had shared with me. It created in me a deep sense of empathy. It made me care for people for who they were.

When was the last time you sat with someone and decided to help them learn something you knew? When was the last time you sat with someone and asked the person to teach you what he or she knows? We think asking for help is a weakness, that it shows people you are stupid or incapable. But that is not true. Asking for help is the greatest show of strength. A sign of a good leader. It shows that you know what you need and where you lack. It shows that you are making an effort to understand, learn, and fill the gap. All the things you would want your kids, your staff at work, the people around you to do, the spotted zebra is not afraid to show that it needs to do these too and leads by example.

Today, I teach my kids to talk to people, to Google, and search for tools to empower their knowledge. If they only learn what everyone else is learning, they will never learn how to find their own unique identity and let it shine. The world needs us to be us.

Unlocking the Anatomy of You

I have an analogy that I use for what this world needs and how society can function at its best. I have given talks on this analogy, but this is the first time I am putting it down in writing. We need to be individuals with a united purpose, like the human body. The body (i.e., humanity), needs to be kept alive and survive in its heathiest form, for the longest possible time, while achieving everything it wants to. The body is made up of different parts—each unique with its own functions. Some are on the outside. They steal the limelight and get noticed a lot, like the skin, the nose, and the eyes. And then there are the vital organs, hidden, no spotlights shining on them, but they are incredibly crucial to the existence of the body. None of the outside would matter if these organs died, like the kidney, the heart, the pancreas, the bile duct, and so on.

I am a minor expert in anatomies because I had many family members including my dad, grandma, uncles, and an older brother—plus a golden retriever—suffer from different types of cancers. This forced me to study the anatomy in my pursuit to try and cure them through natural means, intelligent conversations, suggestions to their physicians, and prayer (best to pray accurately where anatomies are concerned—if I were God, I would ignore lazy generic prayers, so it is a good thing that I am not).

I have digressed as my ADHD often takes me down one rabbit hole after another—welcome to my mind. Anyway, coming back to the different parts of the body—which each one of us are—we are like different organs working together to make the body, which is a representation of society, function in its full capacity. We cannot force everyone to become the heart or the kidney or the pancreas. Unfortunately, society, organizations, governments, and schools do. We decide, for example, that the heart is the vital organ. Imagine if we got everyone to be the heart, how effective and efficient the organization or society would be? We train people to function as the heart, to behave like the heart, to look like the heart.

Unfortunately, a kidney, a pancreas, even the nose, no matter how hard it tries, will never be a heart, and when forced to behave like one, will fail miserably. Every society, like each body, needs its members to function in their respective roles to be a full working body. But we do not train people to be the best version of the member or organ they were meant to be. We do not celebrate the uniqueness of that organ nor its function. We do not want any organ to look different from what we deem as vital. And so, some very critical, unique organs are pronounced failures and unacceptable for simply trying to be themselves. And the organs that try to behave like their more esteemed counterparts fail miserably. We need to allow, empower, and encourage each organ in each body to work to it its best ability and function, and fulfil its destiny.

Yes, people are hard to control. We are unpredictable when left to our own devices. My mother will attest that of me. Many a times, she has been so frustrated, she threatened to sell me in the local market. But, when we function in our uniqueness to the best of our abilities, with each member of society playing his/her part towards a united goal, it works to the greater purpose of making society better—we are all stronger for it. We become better and more progressive. We are more connected. Spotted zebras do not compete to become a better stripped zebra—we compete with ourselves to be the best spotted zebras we were meant to be.

I mentioned how important it is to pursue who you are. But I also mentioned the importance of staying connected. We are parts of a body. While we function as per our individuality, we do not function individually.

What do I mean by this? I heard psychologist Susan Pinker's 2017 TED Talk on the secret to living longer.[5] She conducted a

---

[5] Susan Pinker, 'The secret to living longer may be your social life', *TED*, 2017, https://www.ted.com/talks/susan_pinker_the_secret_to_living_longer_may_be_your_social_life?language=en.

study on the folks at the Italian island of Sardinia, which has over six times as many centenarians as the mainland and ten times as many as North America, to uncover what their secret to longevity was. Surprisingly, it was not the beautiful sun and breeze, nor a healthy diet. It was how connected they were. Apparently close personal relationships and face-to-face interactions could be what helps you hit 100 and live beyond that age.

And Susan describes face-to-face interactions not as how much time you spent with someone. It has nothing to do with inviting them over for a meal and hanging out. It is ensuring that every day you talk to someone, greet someone in the elevator, on the streets, or when you are picking up the morning papers. Touch and go connections count too, as long as you take the time to connect.

The second I heard that, I explained this to my kids, my husband, and all my extended family. I ran out to greet everyone— child, plant, dog, cat, human. I would have conversations with security guards on how their day was, the lady at the café, people in elevators. Most people in my condo saw me and turned around and started walking the other way just to avoid an overly enthusiastic 'Hello, how are you?' In the Singapore culture, this is not normal. Even in the lifts of churches and office building where you see the same person all the time, you avoid saying hello. You refuse to smile or greet them. When you are in the elevator and someone is walking towards you from a distance, you pretend you are pressing the door open for them, but you are actually pressing the 'door close' button. You walk slowly and let your neighbour go ahead so you do not have to talk to them. Well, this apparently shortens our lifespan. We were made to connect. To be social. To be part of something bigger than us.

Be you. Greet people in your unique way. Do not do what society has trained you to do—close your eyes, mind your own business, avoid eye contact, look the other way, and walk in the opposite direction. Do you know why we behave this way? We have been conditioned to not let anything that takes up our time and reduces our efficiency get in the way of our day and what we need to achieve. We have been trained to become robots. It is time to break this cycle of wrongful social conditioning. It is time for you, the spotted zebra, to do the opposite. Stop, slow down, take your time, and talk to everyone you meet. Say hello. Do not fall prey to the self-berating of your mind which will initially keep telling you, 'What are you doing? You're wasting your time. They're going to think you're crazy.' Let them think that. You concentrate on living a rich, long life!

The Spotted Zebra lesson in this is simple. Be true to who you are, no matter how different that makes you. Understand that it is the uniqueness of someone that complements you and completes the picture. If you are all the same—trained to look, behave, and function the same way—you are the same puzzle pieces. Instead, you need to be unique pieces of the same puzzle. Only then can you form the full, beautiful picture. Like the human body, everyone must be the best version of their uniqueness and function in that uniqueness to ensure that society runs as a well-oiled machine.

Learning for Life

My dad got his educational qualification after he beat cancer very late in life while supporting three kids as well as a child whom he had adopted—my beautiful, smart, and incredibly resourceful sister, Grace, who is the favourite aunt of my kids. He had a knack for teaching me life lessons from nature—the ants, the bees, the rivers. There is a lesson to be learned everywhere. Principles to be picked up from those around us. Learning is a survival skill that needs to be cultivated and continuously practiced. It should not be constrained to six years of institutionalization in schools, then in high school, and then in university.

During my years in the big advertising agencies, I would often leave the office to go for a walk, watch a movie, listen to a podcast, to learn new things. These point me to and help me crack big ideas for campaigns. Learning does not stop when you graduate. Learning should literally be lifelong. Education should be fun. And at every point of your life, you should be given the opportunity to apply that learning in a way that helps you make money or a form of currency that feeds and sustains your existence.

The idea that we spend X years to be part of a school system that trains us to become the one thing that gives us a stable job is a shackle that binds us and stops us from growing. It completely curbs risk taking, the desire to try new things, or the guts to try something completely different or something you have developed a new love and passion for at an older age. The notion of lifelong learning is more of an institutionalized catch phrase than a reality. Society does not give you the permission nor the luxury to give up what you are doing, that you are bored out of your wits about, to try something new you love.

In Singapore, via Skills Future initiatives, the government sponsors upskilling for the elderly and those who have lost their jobs. This is amazing, but it also shines the spotlight on a very big problem. Learning is so tightly linked to money that people are only incentivized to learn when there is monetary gain, which is really heart breaking. It is a vicious cycle passed on by the powers that be to families that in turn ingrain it into their children who make decisions on what to pursue in university depending on what would get them a lucrative career that is defined by money rather than passion.

The moment learning becomes something you do purely to earn money, the joy of learning gets taken away. Learning something you love is also taken away. I cannot count the number of people in their 30s and above who have told me that they studied something because their parents approved of and were willing to pay for it. If they did not feel pressured to study it, they would never have gone down that path to begin with.

The reality is that times are changing. The world we live in is changing. In thirty years, according to the billionaire founder of Space X and Tesla, Elon Musk, and Ali Baba founder, Jack Ma, Artificial Intelligence (A.I.) and automated systems would take over most of our jobs[6]. Musk went on to talk about what this means—we will not lack—humans will be on some sort of a government dole because this would be so cheap and affordable with automation. But what I believe we will lack is our identity because human beings identify themselves with their job titles.

Most people value themselves based on what they do, not who they are. In today's society, everyone's identity is plugged into a socio-economic spectrum. This means the greatest crisis humanity will face is not poverty, hunger, or robots taking over our jobs. It is a loss of identity. While our necessities will be provided for, nothing will be able to replace that loss of self-worth.

Think about it. When we introduce ourselves to people, we do it by our name and our position. Or when someone asks you what you do, you automatically take it to mean work. And the asker of the question automatically takes it to mean the same. But what does what we do have to do with our job titles? If we are between jobs, we answer something like 'Oh I used to be an engineer at IBM. I am now just waiting for the right opportunity with a new start-up. That's where the opportunities are.'

We justify our worth and enforce our importance in any conversation by the job title we hold or, in this case, held. But are we not more than our job titles? I challenge you as you read this to try another approach—to go against the norm of the misperceived

---

[6] Karen Gilchrist, Elon Musk: 'A.I. will make jobs kind of pointless—so study this', *CNBC*, 2019, https://www.cnbc.com/2019/08/29/elon-musk-ai-will-make-jobs-kind-of-pointless-so-study-this.html.

societal value of ambition and job titles and introduce yourself as who you are, what you aspire to be outside of work, or something you do that has nothing to do with money.

Who am I? I am a woman who is highly opinionated and not afraid to speak her mind. I am a notorious rule breaker. What do you do? 'Oh, I raise a husband, two humans kids and two fur babies. I support a Filipino woman who thinks she is my helper, but really, she does not do much at home except walk the dogs— we keep her so we can help pay for her son's education and did not have the heart to send her home during the pandemic, back to a country with poor medical care. She is better off with us. I also cook awesome food and am trying some new-age ways to raise my kids for a future that keeps evolving, changing, and is unpredictable—that is part of what I do. Would you like me to continue?'

You're probably laughing and thinking I am crazy now. And yes, if you do the above, you may lose some friends, but you will be a unique, unpredictable conversationist and the person everyone wants to hang out with at every party, and gossip about at the afterparty. And yes, you will find your own identity outside of your work—how can you not when you keep reiterating who you are beyond your job title to yourself and to everyone who asks you what you do?!

Everyone can see you are a zebra. They know everything about the zebra. Now, it is time to talk about your spots.

Chapter 3

The Perfect Teenager who Tried to Take Her Life

This is my hardest chapter to write. My hands are literally shaking, my heart feels like a hand is crushing it, and my eyes are filled with tears. Partly tears of anguish and partly tears of anger. And partly tears of relief because finally this spotted zebra gets to tell her story.

In this chapter, I want to reveal to you a secret. *It is definitely not for the faint-hearted, and one that readers who have gone through similar experiences may find disturbing or traumatizing.* I have spoken about this to less than five people. Well, I may have mentioned about it in passing. You may judge me for it. I am fine with that. You may feel sorry for me. Please do not. They say what does not kill you makes you stronger. In my case, I literally could have died on several occasions, but I did not—and I am stronger for it.

An Unlikely Predator

The story starts with my godfather. My godfather was a very charismatic man. He was a close family friend. When my parents converted to Christianity when I was seven, he mentored and discipled us. He was the founder and religious leader of a large Christian organization. And today, when I look back at some of the things he taught us, I realize how cult-like it was. And how much his personal agenda, ambition, and desires shaped the organization. There were a great number of genuine followers who thought he was pointing the way to God. And then there was a very small group of opportunists who formed his inner circle, and as with every cult, went along with him hoping to share a portion of the wealth and power he was amassing along the way.

As with all religious organizations, he started with seemingly sincere objectives—starting with a revival that helped people like my parents have real, honest, and personal encounters with God.

As a seven-year-old who had seen my dad miraculously escape death and cancer, and always had been curious about the supernatural world, I was drawn to him. And when he and his wife decided that I was to be their godchild whom they would mentor and look out for as a second set of parents, my parents thought it was a good idea. He had a following of hundreds of thousands from all over the world and was a famous published writer. Today, he would be likened to the motivational speaker, author, and influencer, Jay Shetty—minus the good looks. He always seemed to have the best interests of everyone at heart. And he spoke with so much wisdom and insight, everyone in his circle of influence (believe me, it was far and wide at a time of no social media) considered his words the ultimate counsel from God. So, you can imagine . . . what could go wrong?!

Well, he was a paedophile. And he groomed me since I was a child so he could have his way with me. It was the pre-Google era. It started when I was eleven—the little intimate, inappropriate touches which I had no idea were inappropriate. Even though they made me uncomfortable, I trusted him—he was a supposed to be a godly man. Everyone believed him and thought he was good. Who was I, a child, to doubt that? The abuse increased with each passing year. Once again, this was a time before Google and social media. I lived a very 'protected' life. No exposure to sex.

My parents gave me the sex talk, but it was a very sanitized version. I had no clue what a paedophile was. I was not exposed to mass media and advertising. I was innocent and completely ignorant to all that was happening to me. And he had a way of doing things in secret while using God and the Bible to console me that it was all right and that I should keep his behaviour a secret because I was in the wrong. So, at the tender age of fourteen, when he raped me for the first time, I did not say a word. I remember his hand over my mouth, and after he was done, he said, 'There, you are now officially mine.' I was very quiet that day. No matter what he had said and how he had justified his actions, I felt dirty and condemned. I bathed so many times and kept washing my skin with Dettol.

I wanted to tell somebody, but I could not. His family was also very close to mine. They had been supporting and helping my parents for years. There was a false sense of obligation that if I ratted on him, I was doing something wrong—I was betraying a good person. He would repeatedly drill into me how important the work he was put on earth to do was. He hung this subconscious threat over my head that if I said anything to anyone, I would be a tool of the devil, destroying that good work. That all of this would be my fault.

Can you image being fourteen, sexually abused, and having to bear the weight of thousands of souls perishing and going to hell should I accidentally mention what he was doing to me to someone? Today, when I look back, I think, what a load of hogwash! How could I have believed that?! Then I look at my fourteen-year-old son, despite all his exposure to social media (and the fact that I made sure from the age of four that both my children understood what a paedophile was and the whole stranger-danger and wrong touch concept), he is still so clueless and immature about so many things. And I think, I did not even have the support and knowledge he has when I was exposed to an extremely manipulative man who knew exactly that and took advantage of me and my family.

The worst part, thanks to his meticulously calculated grooming, despite all his actions and violent abuse, I was repeatedly made to believe that the whole situation was my fault. He had convinced me it was.

If I was seen talking to any boys in his presence, he would feel the need to teach me a lesson—a whole lot of verbal berating and brutal sexual abuse. In public, he was this benevolent, kind, charismatic leader. In private, he genuinely seemed to think I was God's gift to him to do with as he pleased.

I would have these dreams of escaping and running away from him. And I shared them with him initially, because he was a big believer that God spoke through dreams. I hoped that he would understand that I needed to get away when he heard my dreams. Instead, he interpreted them to his advantage each time, saying it was my subconscious fighting against God's will.

Each time it made me feel like I was a sinner. Someone who was going against God's will. The irony was, I genuinely enjoyed reading my Bible. I liked praying. But now, this man was using God to his advantage, and it made me think if this was God, he must hate me so much to want me to go through this. I genuinely thought if this was God's will, my life had no value.

The worst part was the double life I had to live, pretend in front of my parents and friends that I was fine. Life was good. Pretend I was happy when I was with my friends. After a while, I was not pretending. I completely convinced myself that this was the best life I could have. And I had to make the most of it. And this was when my ADHD started manifesting at its maximum. I would talk to myself and answer my own questions.

I never had a night's peaceful sleep when I stayed with my godparents, partly because of the nightmares and partly because I was afraid of him coming into my room at night. I would throw myself into endless activities to keep my mind active and my heart from feeling the pain, fear, and perpetual sense of danger. I was able to completely separate logic from feeling—I honestly think even Star Trek's Vulcan Academy would have immediately accepted me as their prized human student.

People who wanted to score points with him constantly carried news of my whereabouts, if I was with boys, or groups of girls my age doing something 'suspicious' (and by this, I mean all teenage activities), any overly friendly interaction with the opposite sex, or simply seen as having too much 'secular' fun. Now, I have to say, while I enjoyed a good time and certainly knew how to have fun (ask my friends—they will say I was never short of ideas), I always did well academically and in sports because I found so much stability and peace in studying, taking exams and engaging in physical competitions. Because I had convinced myself that this whole thing was my fault, I spent many days of my life in a state of penance—fasting, praying, trying to lead the perfect life. I had to get As. I had to be great at sports. I could not think any evil thoughts for people or be mean to them no matter how mean they were—okay, I always had a witty streak— and sometimes something snarky would escape my mouth—but that was more as a display of my stand-up comedy prowess, not so much my evil intentions. Not all religious fanatics took kindly to this, I discovered.

I had a few short-term boyfriends my age—well, more like friends who were boys. I needed this to feel normal. And I have ADHD, so a relationship never lasted long. Either way, as soon as word got out, I was punished, and it quickly ended. In some cases, the guys were secretly threatened. Word always got out. My godfather was a highly connected person. I did not know this then, but he always had people watching my every move. He had spies everywhere because he was afraid, I might accidentally say something. All the time. There was no trust. Only control. And then there were the people who were jealous of the fact that he was my godfather and kept trying to get me into trouble with him or wanted to curry favour with a man of such influence, so they took joy in reporting my every movement to him.

'Oh, she's with this girl who often shoplifts. They shouldn't be friends.' Or 'I saw her hanging out with a friend at a Buddhist temple. People are going to think she's a heathen.' Or 'She was crossing the road with this boy who kept pinching her cheeks.' Now, there was truth in this last one. But he was my cousin. None of them knew the consequences of their complaints, but each time, I ended up being taught a lesson that broke me just a bit more.

Failing at Dying

I remember when I was sixteen, there was an episode at a church camp. It was the holidays. During holidays, I stayed with my godparents. I played a prank by calling from the front office and pretending there was a fire. I tricked some church folks into evacuating their rooms. I was a teenager, bored out of my wits, wanting to do stuff people my age did. I also went for swims, danced to some music someone from the camp played at the pool, and became good friends with the person who drove me to the venue.

Till today I have no clue what reports reached his ears but all I remember is the price I paid. The berating and abuse were so bad, I stayed curled in the corner of the couch wishing I was dead.

It was still the holidays, and I went home one of the nights and took two packs of Panadol. That is the other thing—in this home, there was no medication. So, I had to go to a pharmacy to get some. I was so afraid about going to a doctor because there was an unspoken rule about trusting God for healing, I had to put on a hoodie and sneak into the pharmacy to get my meds. I can imagine how dodgy I must have looked to the pharmacist. Well, I got my two packs.

All I remember was popping the Panadol, all of them. Then feeling drowsy. I slept. And then I saw nothing. Except the voice of my cousin Nixon calling me and asking me if I was okay. A recurring dream. I had no clue what was happening. I woke up two days later. My room was a bit stinky. My body was weak. No one seemed to have checked on me. My godparents were busy at religious conferences. I picked myself up, my body aching like crazy, and ran to the toilet with bad diarrhoea. My urine was almost bloody and cloudy. I looked like crap, and my kidney was hurting like crazy.

I bathed with whatever strength I could muster, all the while drinking down the shower water from sheer thirst. After that, I went to the kitchen, and stuffed myself with bread, butter, and some minestrone soup I found in the slow cooker. I was starving. I sat there with zero feelings, thinking to myself 'God must really love me to want me alive. Or He must hate me to make me continue with my torture.' Whichever it was, I certainly sucked at dying.

That was not the first time I tried to take my life. At the age of twenty, things got so bad, I started sleeping in my car at night when I visited them. This was in Kuala Lumpur. It was not the safest thing to do. To my godparents, I was staying with a friend. But I would have braved any danger compared to the abuse I was being put through.

The Final Blow

The hardest blow came when I found out my godmother knew about it all along. Or at least I suspected she did. She herself was a victim, happy that the focus was now turned to someone other than her, so she let it happen without doing anything.

I did not know which was worse—to be repeatedly sexually and verbally abused and controlled and thinking I deserved it and not be able to do anything about it, or to be betrayed by another woman who knew what I was going through and thought 'better her than me.'

My godmother's mom would come and visit sometimes and mentioned to her that my godfather was physically too close to me and often touched me. But instead of doing something about it, she got her mom to pack up and go home.

One day, when my godmother was giving me a ride to church, she started telling me about how she caught my godfather being intimate with a teenage girl but forgave him because he apologized, and said he was a changed man. I was sitting there thinking she must know something, if not, why would she be telling me this. I wanted to tell her that I needed help, but I could hear my godfather's voice in my head saying that if I were to say anything, it would all come crashing down and the many lost souls would be my fault. I kept quiet and looked at her hoping she would say something like 'I know you're in trouble. This is what you can do.' But she did not.

Then, one day, when my godfather had me pinned under him, I am pretty sure she walked in on us, and I am pretty sure she saw me looking at her for help. She turned around and walked away. That day again, something inside me died. Hope. Like a candlelight, it was blown out.

I bore with her berating, insulting, name calling. She had thrown things at me and accused me of taking things in the house that I had never touched. She complained to my mom I was madly in love with and dating a guy she caught me with a few times. My mom looked at her and said, 'The guy is literally her cousin, they grew up together, are close in age and are good friends.' At that point, I told myself that she was just a paranoid godmother who was trying her best to guide me and show me love in her own way. I really did think the best of her. Also, they had two amazing kids who literally were my only source of comfort in that mad, dysfunctional cult headquarters of a home. But that day when I caught her turning away, I realized she hated me because I was the object of her husband's lust but did not want to help me escape from it either because I was also the focus of his abuse.

It just drove me to a very dark place, and this time, I took every medication I could get my hands on. I visited friends and stole their meds—cough syrup, antihistamine, pain killers. I popped them with a vengeance on a day when I knew my godparents were away and my parents thought I was camping and could not be reached. Everyone I knew thought I was camping, so no one came to check in or look for me. Thank God for the lack of connectivity back in the day. You could just disappear, and no one would know.

Despite taking so many meds, a day later, I woke up with what felt like a massive hangover. I remember opening my eyes and not being able to see anything for a few minutes. And I thought, 'Oh shit, I have made myself blind instead of dying.' And then the vision came back, blurry at first, and then clear. And then I ran to the toilet and threw up. For three days, I was lying in bed in between throwing up. All I could do was suck on frozen Ribena. My godmother came in, saw me throwing up, then ran out of the house.

Hope from a Stranger

A day later, a lady drove by. Till today, I am not sure if my godmother had sent her. But she drove by the house—an elderly Indian woman who looked respectable and affluent. She stood at the gate and shouted, 'Uma, can you dress up and come with me? I'm here to help you.'

I got dressed, and for some strange reason, forsook the idea of 'stranger danger' and jumped in her car. She knew my name. And in a very, very long time, she was the first person who had offered to help me. That was enough for me, especially after I had been so sick from trying to take my life.

I got in her car. She looked at me. I could not quite make out what she was thinking. I was still nursing a headache and a combination of hunger and nausea. She said she was going to drop me outside a building. I had to go up to level 8 or 9 and knock on the door. And someone will help me. She said, 'Do not tell anyone you're getting help. Christians do not take too kindly to people seeing psychologists. But you need help. And he will help you.'

When she mentioned psychologist, I got scared. I thought of the movies I had seen and imagined myself in a straitjacket, strapped to a seat, and electrocuted by a shrink. I wanted to run away and hide, but I thought to myself, I have had so many bad things happen and have survived two suicide attempts. What would one more do?

I remember walking into his room. It was small but well decorated. He was a Eurasian man, a lot younger than I expected, in his late 30s. He smiled and said, 'I know you're from a highly religious community. So, I guess seeing me is taboo. But I am here to help you. You look really sick, were you trying to kill yourself?' I remember he laughed. I was not sure whether he was joking. But I had no reaction.

I remember sitting there silently. Not nodding. Really not saying much to anything he said. I did not know what to say. I had been taught my entire life on how to behave, what to say, what to do. The only time I express myself is in my creativity when I am writing plays, which are usually fantastical in nature with other world creatures, aliens and space, songs, singing, acting, or directing—I love creating and reading about creation through physics. Seeing a psychologist meant I had mental problem, and back in the day, it was shameful. You were shunned, looked down upon for having mental health problems.

Funnily, when the psychologist told me that he was agnostic, I felt at peace. I felt I could trust him. I felt like the God I had perceived to be cruel was not allowed in this conversation. He decided—since I was not talking—to run some tests. This I loved. I love tests, and whilst undergoing the tests, I spoke more freely to him. I cannot remember much of what I said as I was focusing on the tests, but I remember feeling free, comfortable and him being genuine and kind.

I came back a second day after the tests to get my test results. I could see a mixture of anguish and amusement on his face. He said, 'I am going to be straight with you. I can tell when someone is being abused. Physically and sexually. The signs are all there. And you have all of them. I have an obligation to report you to the Malaysian Welfare Department. But I won't. That system is so messed up, it will kill you. You will be twenty-one next year. The first test I ran was to check if you have any mental conditions. You were exceptionally quiet, and at times, I thought you had spaced out on me. You have ADHD. Highly functional despite having it. But you have it. I do not know if you've had it all the while or if it surfaced as part of your body's survival instincts. But it seems to have kept you alive.'

He laughed and added, 'The second test we ran, that was an IQ test. You are exceptionally smart and exceptionally perceptive. You have capabilities most people do not. Which is why it pains me to see someone so smart and capable think so poorly of one's value.'

Then he stopped and said, 'I usually listen and do not talk. But I do not have any more sessions with you. So, listen carefully. Your life is your own. Stop living it out of fear and shame or guilt and remorse. Live it for yourself. Ignore what everyone else says and live for yourself. You are a smart girl. You know how to do that. Break away from the people hurting you and live for yourself.'

As I walked out of that room that day, his words echoed in my mind. 'Live for yourself.' I decided that day that I was never going to try and take my own life. I was going to live. Not by someone else's terms but by my own.

At the age of eighteen, I had met a young boy four years older than me named Colin. We needed a bassist for the church band,

and he showed up. He was kind and genuine and we were good friends. At the age of twenty, I realized he was interested in me.

So, I decided to test the water and told him what I was experiencing. I started gathering evidence. Letters my godfather had written. Colin was so frightened when he heard what I was going through. I thought he was going to run away. I thought he would think I am crazy and making up stories about such a well-respected man. But he hugged me and started making plans on how he could help me escape from my situation.

Long story short, it took me a whole lot of courage, a new boyfriend whom I am now married to for twenty-one years and have children with, and some detailed planning to escape my godfather, a very influential, well-connected man.

It also took prayer. And while you may wonder how I can still believe in God, I genuinely believe the God I thought to be cruel enabled my escape.

I remember the night I decided to pack and leave. I decided I was going to make my way back to my parents. I still could not bring myself to tell them everything as I still felt it was all my fault. I was young and in an abusive relationship where I was physically and sexually abused for seven years, all the while being lied to and told this was what God wanted for me, this was what I deserved, and if I blew the whistle on the situation, I would be destroying lives.

That night, my godmother came back early from a council meeting, saw me pack up, and called my godfather. He came back and started using every means in the book of cult manipulation to persuade me. Threats, guilt, anguish, begging. I just let the words of the psychologist flood over me, 'Live for yourself.' And stood my ground.

What triggered me to leave was my godfather telling me that God had told him that his wife was going to die, and he was going to marry me. This completely had me freaked. I was not going to be an accomplice to a murder.

That night, as I stood outside the gate with my bags packed, with my godfather begging me to come home, two of his associate pastors came over to see what was happening. He tried to have them convince me to stay but they got suspicious because of my sheer desperation. I have always been a level-headed girl, always compliant and happy. But there was strength and determination in me that day.

He insisted that we go in and talk it out. I agreed under one condition: after the talk with the two pastors, he would take me to my parents. He agreed. Then he took me to a room, threatened me and abused me. Then he begged and apologized. And then when he realized I would not change my mind, he begged me not to tell anyone. I remember telling myself this is it. I will never let him touch me again. Ever.

In my bag, I had packed all evidence of the relationship. Letters from him. I hid it because if ever I needed to prove this had happened, I would have it. And boy was I glad I did. Because otherwise no one would have believed me. But I decided I was going to be selfish, think of me, and get out. And it was the best thing I had done. Looking back, it felt a bit like leaving a mafia ring.

It took me months to get over what I had experienced and tell my parents what had happened. Eventually, word got out and the pastors needed evidence to get him to step down. I shared the letters, and when they accused me, I did not even know how to defend myself. All his followers started pointing fingers and blaming me—the young girl, the temptress, the one he had taken care of, who was turning her back on him.

The week after I left, my godmother came to my home. Despite knowing all that had happened, she begged me to come back so things could go back to normal. My mom was about to grab her by the collar and throw her out.

I am just glad that back in the day there was no social media. But if there were, my truth might have come out. I would have felt more empowered by knowledge and understood that I was innocent in all of this. I realized no one is evil alone; systems and people empower them. When I left, his followers and people who were on his payroll, despite knowing what had happened, gave him reports of where I was. He desperately tried to find me so that he could use me to turn the narrative in his favour. And when all else failed, he blamed me. I got a letter from the church excommunicating me. Despite being the victim, I was villainized. I remembered thinking, should not the church be a place of protection, a sanctuary? Should they not pick me up and pay for my counselling? Instead, they chucked me out.

Two very senior religious leaders took advantage of the situation to throw my godfather out and take over his role of leadership over the religious organization. One even wrote a book about the situation, barely knowing any of the facts, describing the situation as incest, calling me a co-conspirator, and painting the most erroneous account in a book full of false reporting that he and his wife labelled as spiritual guidance. It was my parents and Colin who counselled me, picked me up, and encouraged me.

I was not totally out of the woods. Years of abuse takes time to recover and heal from. There were many nights when I would wake up thinking it was all my fault and life was not worth living. I would hold a knife to my wrist and hide it when my mom walked in. She would look worried but not say much. She would just sit with me and pray for me through the night. She would encourage me and remind me I have a great destiny. My mom and dad constantly reminded me that I was brilliant.

I never told anyone about the psychologist. It was only years later that I would find the courage to own my ADHD. I used to be so ashamed of it. And no one knows I took an IQ test and scored high except my husband, and now you, dear reader. But frankly, I think IQ tests are a very Western, skewed, one-dimensional way to put intelligence in a box. It did nothing to save me from the situation I was in for seven years.

But as I mentioned at the start of this chapter, do not feel sorry for me. What did not kill me made me courageous. I took away some very powerful lessons from that situation. And each time I look back, I learn something new. I have learned that the bad things you go through continue to teach you and make you better even years after you have walked out of the situation.

The Healing in Acceptance

I learned that those moments when I am completely lost in my own thoughts, creating new things, lose sight of time, and start ignoring everyone around me—it is part of my ADHD. I used to have a million ideas like bouncing balls trying to get out of a door at the same time, but never succeeding because they are constantly growing and bumping into each other. I learned techniques to control that and become an expert communicator who distilled difficult concepts into the simplest and easiest, most understandable articulations. I learned that my inability to sleep was not just fear of my godfather, it was also something positive—my mind unable to stop thinking of new ideas. Even my ability to separate my emotions from my logic very cleanly and deliberately was a strength. Someone can hurt me deeply, and instead of blowing up, I have the ability to walk away from the situation and analyze it. Only days later will the emotions follow, and I will be in my toilet, curled up and crying alone. But now I can gather myself, put the two together and make good decisions versus just being guided by logic or emotion.

I need to use the same cubicle in the toilet even if the rest are empty. And I need to sit at the same seat at church, at home when watching TV, or when visiting the library. And when I go to a restaurant, I need to sit at a place where I feel my back is against the wall and I am looking at the door. I hate parking indoors and hold my breath in lifts and the MRT until the door opens. I do not like being touched by strangers, even accidentally. And I need to be officially introduced to people or have a logical 'task' to execute to talk to people. And my mind completely blanks out and erases people who are insignificant or have hurt me. I remember animals in detail and recognize one chicken from another even when they look alike. But I cannot do that with people. Maybe because I trust animals more. Coffee makes me calm and helps me sleep. Alcohol doesn't make me drowsy; it makes me sharp. My boss at Ogilvy used to bring out the whisky at 3 a.m. when we had to stay back for late night pitches because he realized how focused that helped me stay. Now, when people look at these behaviours and think I am mental, I proudly say, yes, I have clinical ADHD. Some think I am joking. Some go, 'Oh, that explains it.' Either way, I do not care. At least I know why I behave the way I do. I have come to understand me and my value.

The lesson from the spotted zebra is that we must acknowledge our mental state and conditions even if others shun them. Even though I never talked about it to anyone then, I started reading up on it. There was very little material available, and remember, there was no Google. But I started looking for similarities in others and talked to them. But the most helpful thing was, the second someone put a name to it and helped me see what it was, I was able to understand I was different, it took time, but I came to accept and embrace my difference. It is not easy to give yourself permission to be different. We have to do it to be our full selves. And when our difference gets in the way of us achieving things, we need to embrace the challenge, call it 'game on', overcome the hurdles. And as I did this, I started turning my ADHD into my strength. I could stay up all night and work on projects, plays, and campaigns and go to work the next day with just as much energy and strength; no one could tell I had stayed up the whole night.

I learned to let go and not hold grudges because I could logically analyze what happened to me without having my emotions get in the way. And when my feelings finally caught up, because I had logically analyzed it, all I needed to do was allow the emotions to flow and pass through, and then I was okay. Sometimes, this was harder to do. People never understood me and thought I was being cold. But I was not. I merely processed things differently.

Having been the victim of a paedophile in a culture where it was shameful to be a young girl in my shoes, where the victim was blamed, made me angry at what was wrong with the society and want to change it. It also made me brave and strong. It built in me compassion for women and men who had gone through abuse. It still has adverse effects—when I see graphic films or read novels on abuse like the movie *Sleepers* and the book *Kite Runner*, I need to physically throw up. But it also put in me a desire to save and rescue girls and boys in this situation; to protect others even when they are total strangers; to ensure there is sufficient and correct education.

My story did not end here. Walking out was just the start. I was in my early twenties. I had lost my sense of dignity and self-confidence. I was angry about what had happened to me. But I channelled that anger to change the world for the better. I became a journalist with the desire to write articles that helped empower young girls and gave them self-confidence. It made me stop living for others and start living for myself. This also meant rediscovering who God is outside of all the things that were taught to me by my godfather and his cult. I promised myself I will do what I believe is right; to never let someone else influence my decisions; to be responsible for my own life irrespective of what people thought of me.

I think the biggest hurdle that stops us from becoming who we are is that we esteem someone else's opinion above the truth we know inside. It is your life, do not let someone else control it. It takes courage to stand against societal norm and decide to take steps in the opposite direction. My life for seven years was in shambles because I let someone else control it and thought about what everyone else believed to be the right thing do. But when I came out of the situation, I promised myself from now on I am making my own decisions. I do not care what anyone says or thinks. I am going to do what I believe to be right. And yes, I have done stupid things along the way. Some I regret. But at least every night when I lay my head to rest, there is this sense of freedom and liberty. I do not know how to describe it. For seven years, I felt like a slave. But when I walked out of that situation, and even though I had so much fear and people were insulting me and hurling mud and pulling down my reputation unfairly, inside me was this inexplicable joy, gratitude, and a great sense of freedom and liberty. Now I knew what it was like to be a nation liberated—achieving its independence.

I remember when I was a young journalist, I spent some time in Hong Kong, covering the handover back to China, the development of a youth choir, and the classical music scene. It was some of the best months of my life. And one of the persons I interviewed was an old composer and conductor, Sergiu Comissiona[7]. He was born in Romania when it was under the Russian regime. He was a brilliant conductor who knew from the age of four that he wanted to conduct. His talent was spotted very early by the communist regime, and he was sent for training. As a young conductor, he met and fell in love with a famous ballet dancer. But they could never leave the country together for holidays because the communist regime feared they would defect. It got too much for them and they filed to officially exit Romania. The communist regime came down hard on them. All their property and money were seized. They had to live in secret in the basement of close friends. The US government put

---

[7] https://en.wikipedia.org/wiki/Sergiu_Comissiona

pressure on Romania to let them go, and they finally were able to escape Romania.

As we sat in the hotel room with a gorgeous harbour view backdrop in Hong Kong, I held the fragile hands of him and his wife. We cried together, as he whispered to me peering straight in my eye, 'No price is too great for freedom.' I knew what that was like. I remembered my escape from the lion's den.

When you try and fit into a normalcy mould, you are a slave to society's expectations. When you push against it to be you, you become liberated. And if you, like me, have been trapped in a bad situation, do not hide from it. Do not pretend it is not happening or that it is good, and you need to go through it. Break free now. No matter what it costs you.

Another thing that I learned was the importance of understanding what bad looks like. We live in a society that loves to censor something that is bad or politically incorrect. My parents, religion, church, society—everyone decided young girls need to be shielded from topics around 'sex' and 'bad sex'. The thinking is, if you hide them from it, they will not encounter it. Now that is what predators hope society would do. Ignorance and a lack of knowledge is the biggest trap, the greatest threat to safety.

I let my kids watch movies which have rape, pillage, and plunder. I sit with them and explain what it is, what the motivations are, and why people do it. Of course, I skip all the graphic bits. But they know something bad is happening. I explain that bad things happen in this world. And the best protection they can have is knowing what it looks like and know when and how to escape from it. I also taught them how to stand up for people in trouble and how to get the help they need without landing themselves in trouble.

And then I used my story to teach them an important lesson. While society and religious organizations set aside people who have gone through experiences like mine as broken or spoiled goods, we are not. We have experiences that are unique, that can be used to protect others from similar situations and restore people who have been through these situations. We have the power to create environments and policies that would ensure this does not happen to others. The spotted zebra knows that ugly things that you experience is not the end of your life. It is an opportunity to learn and make more of your life. It is an experience that makes you stronger, better, and more empathetic.

And then I taught them the most important lesson: no matter what bad things people do to you, no matter how much they hurt you, do not let that hurt hold you back. Let it go. If you keep staying angry with them for what they have done to you, they will continue to have a hold over your life. But if you let it go, look forward and move on and reach for your future, grateful you are given the opportunity to continue your life, and be the best version of you, that is the best way to get back at them. The people who tried to hurt you will suffer their worst when they see all their attempts to destroy your life have failed. The best revenge is a life well lived. When Hollywood, Bollywood, and Korea make movies on getting back at the perpetrator, you do the opposite. Let go of the past. Turn the pain into life lessons. Help those in similar situations as you were in. And live your best life ever!

Chapter 4

The Journalist Who was Not Street-smart

I would like to tell you that I got smarter from my experience, but honestly, even after walking away, I was not. The guilt and shame of what I had gone through in my teenage years did not make me strong overnight. In fact, I was so ashamed to have gone through it. I was embarrassed at first that I had a label, a clinical condition. People I knew were calling me a slut and a whore years after I found the courage to walk out of that bad situation, and it became public. That is a lot to bear when you are twenty-one. So, even though I chose to move forward, people were still trying to fling mud at me.

A Rookie Learning the Ropes

I was not exactly the most street-smart person. I was thoroughly protected despite growing up in and being exposed to different cultures in Malaysia, Australia, and New Zealand. I found my calling and satisfaction in my role as a journalist. I guess, earnestness and innocence is a great lure, and I had many wonderful journalist friends who did their best to teach me the ropes and help me. The Star was easily one of the best places I worked at. Well, it was my first proper job. It taught me the foundations of doing great research during pre-Google days. You had to go to a library and look at past news clippings and read through all of them for days. Or find contacts in different organizations who could fax (yes, it was the days of fax machine) you information. It had a low-tech espionage feel to it. Being a journalist makes you incredibly resourceful. You have to be able to make calls, find sources in the weirdest of places, and if you worked on a Sunday in the political news desk, you needed phone numbers of ministers so you could contact them, go to the golf courses where they were teeing off, and between chomping on thin slices of banana cake and Teh Tarik (tea with condensed milk), discuss their political ambitions and gossip in the Malaysian political grapevine so you could go back and write your report. It was all very exciting. But soon I went from the political news beat to the features desk. Here the excitement was less, but the glamour factor was more.

During my five-year tenure as a journalist, I had the numbers of Malaysian ministers and their bodyguards on my Nokia banana mobile phone which I had won at a Nokia Press Night. I had gotten into a fight with Kenny G about his hair, touched Ricky Martin's right butt at his insistence—this was before he came out, interviewed Sammy Hagar from Van Halen who cried on my shoulders about his ill-treatment and his new baby. I spent weeks camping in different jungles with famous photographers and an Indiana Jones look-alike and got shouted at on national television by a minister. I went to karaoke with the APAC head of Pfizer. Every story I wrote was new, unique, and different. I even won an award for a story I did on environmental battles fought on Penang Hill without setting foot on the hill.

I was constantly challenged to do the impossible. I had teenagers threaten to kill me when the story of their vices was out, and their parents grounded them. A story I wrote got two kids unfairly kicked out of school, and I had to beg a colleague to speak to the education minister to help them out. Everything turned out for good. And I had parents call me to ask for advice on their children's future. I felt inadequate but always gave them the best answer I knew with honesty.

I genuinely enjoyed writing feature pieces that could entertain, educate, and even change the way people thought about things. I loved talking to people. I would sit with those I interviewed and cry as they shared painful, intimate tales and laugh as they talked about the craziest experiences. These got me so many front-page stories, scoops, and contacts, it filled my heart with joy and in so many ways restored my confidence and my self-image. My weakness became my strength. My innocence became what people trusted, it made them want to protect me, help me, and let me be the one to tell their stories. Every story was different and unique. Every assignment taught me something new.

I remember my first assignment. No one told me I had to check for assignments the night before. And my first assignment was to get some human-interest stories at Batu Caves during Thaipusam. Now, let me explain a little about this festival. Thaipusam is celebrated by the Hindu Tamil community on the full moon in the Tamil month of *Thai*[8]. *Kavadi Attam* or Kavadi dance is a ceremonial act of devotional sacrifice through dance, food offerings, and bodily self-mortification, including piercing their bodies with spears. It is often performed by devotees during the festival of Thaipusam in honour of the Hindu god Murugan. The kavadi is a semi-circular, decorated canopy supported by a wooden rod that the pilgrims carry on their shoulders to the temple. Batu Caves is the focal point of the Tamil festival of Thaipusam in Malaysia[9]. It is a limestone hill that has a series of caves and cave temples in Gombak, Selangor, Malaysia. The cave is one of the most popular Hindu shrines outside of India, dedicated to Murugan.

---

[8] https://en.wikipedia.org/wiki/Thaipusam

[9] https://en.wikipedia.org/wiki/Batu_Caves

So, you can imagine how crazy I looked showing up in white high heels and a long skirt to the most crowded religious festival, full of perverts who try to feel up women. I had to park about five kilometres away and walk to Batu Caves because the roads were closed to make room for the pilgrims. I had no idea what to expect, and honestly, I was terrified when I got there. The sun was beating hard on me, and my feet were killing me.

Fortunately, I found a young Scandinavian man who looked decent, so I mostly stuck with him to protect myself. And he became my first human-interest story: a Scandinavian who had come to Malaysia and converted to Hinduism, finally completing a pilgrimage, and carrying the kavadi and going through the Hindu procession.

I always imagined journalists as tough people, street-smart and brave. Honestly, I was not any of these things. I was scared, had no clue what a good story looked like, and worked very hard to find out about topics I had zero knowledge of, so that I could ask the right questions. But I learned early that when you do not know something, admit your ignorance and ask for help. Admitting this lack was what made CEOs and people in high places and low places (security guards, receptionists) give me the information I often needed to get a scoop or an inside contact. People genuinely want to help. You just need to be humble and admit that you need their help.

This was a big spotted zebra learning for me. When I joined the Star, I was tempted to do what was expected. To never admit defeat. Hide my ignorance. Avoid asking stupid questions. I did the opposite. I asked questions at the risk of being seen as a greenhorn, a noob. I was also shy. I can hear people I know reading this line and wondering if it is even possible. You see me today and you will think that is impossible. But I am telling you, no one is born brave. We all have our fears. Some of us hide it better than others.

But when you think about it, why should you have to hide your fear and ignorance? Why not show it, ask for help, and learn from those who have gone before you? Should not life be an exchange of strengths—those who are good at things you are not, teaching you how to become good at these things; and you teaching people who are not as good at the things you have mastered on how they can up their game?

I have to say that journalism was the perfect job for a young girl who had lost her self-confidence and courage and desperately needed a place to take her time to hide and slowly blossom. It made me brave and strong at my own pace, on my own terms. A bonus was that my mother loved how she got all the scoops on Malaysian politics long before the newspapers were out. My dad would sit with me and spend hours chatting about life lessons I learned from the people I had met. Journalists are very poor in terms of salary. It was appalling how little money I was making. But back in the day, I also got ex-gratia every month because the Star was doing well. That and all the freebies you get from being a journo got me through the month.

But I was rich in every other way—from the many different experiences I got to live, the people I met, and the stories I heard. These things made me feel rich in my heart, mind, and experience. They were things money cannot buy. I felt in those few years that I had lived many lives. And this job prepared me for my next job in advertising, which was full of sharks in the water.

Taking an Unexpected Path

I chanced upon advertising by accident. Prior to going into advertising, I worked in PR for a short while, but I was bad at it. I spoke my mind to clients, told them exactly what I thought. Then I got a temp job to fill in for an account servicing person in a big advertising agency. The copywriter wrote such bad copy,

I had to keep rewriting everything. This was when the Executive Creative Director (ECD), who happened to be a distant relative, decided I would make a better copywriter. My dad fell ill in the middle of all of this. Being daddy's girl in every way, this was one of my most painful life experiences.

I quit my job to look after my dad. My amazing husband, Colin, was fine with me quitting my job, and held our family together financially. During this time, I freelanced as a script writer for a children's animation series. Watching my strong, handsome, kind dad's body be ravaged by cancer broke my heart. It was the year 2000. He was fifty-seven and had pancreatic cancer. He died that year. I had gone through great tragedy as a teenager, but this loss broke my heart. I loved my dad. He was my favourite human on this planet. He was everything my godfather was not.

Remember when I said that I had decided to rediscover God for myself? I stayed a Christian. I looked for God in the Bible. But a big part of what made me stay a Christian was my parents, the way they loved me unconditionally, shielded, protected, and prayed for me through my darkest moments. They are the best example of Christians in my life. I remember when my dad passed away. My mind processed what had happened. But my emotions only kicked in three days later and after being cool, collected, and composed and helping my family organize the funeral, I broke down hard. My husband stood there and watched and said, 'I wondered when you were going to cry. Finally. This is good. This is truly good.'

I still cry when I talk about him. You never get over such great love. You just get used to it. I loved hanging with my dad. After what happened with my godfather, my dad gave me a strong sense of safety.

After my dad passed away, we left for Singapore. My husband got a chance to set up the branch for his KL-based software house here. And with great hope, I left an environment that held so many painful memories to start afresh. This was an opportunity to discover a new me, away from the entanglements of the past. Away from the trauma and reminders of having lost a loved one.

It was the clean slate I needed. We sold our cars, packed up our lives in two suitcases, and gave away everything precious. This included my original Star Wars movie posters and memorabilia, my many shoes, and our beautiful Golden Retriever, Curry, whom my brother and sister-in-law adopted.

In Singapore, I accidentally chanced upon the world of advertising in all its glory. I was not filling in. This time, I was hired to be the copywriter. Once again, I felt the same way. I was intimidated by the fact that everyone had gone to fancy advertising schools. I was merely an ex-journalist. I had studied theology and political science. I had no clue about copywriting or the glitzy world of advertising. I felt like such a fake, but I always asked for help. I kept asking senior folks for their opinions on my work, asking how and what I could do better. Some laughed and did not give me the time of the day, still I kept at it.

But in my first year of advertising, I won a few awards and made copywriter of the year. I can assure you that it was not because I was brilliant but because I asked for help and admitted to things I did not know. I was also hungry. I really wanted to win and excel at this. I kept asking for help even when the reception was not as welcoming. Unlike Malaysia, in Singapore, people were a lot more cynical to young ones who wanted to learn. The culture and attitude to help was different. But I valued the life lessons. I learned the power of persistence.

And this was my spotted zebra lesson. More than being all-suave and all-knowing, it is amazing how far vulnerability and humility can get you. Even the people who do not think you are good enough can be persuaded to help when you persistently knock on their door, even if it is just to get rid of you. And when you persistently do something, you cannot help but get better at it. Society tells you some people have it, and some people just do not. Give up and move on to something different. But you must never let someone's limited knowledge of you and encounter with you define who you are and what you are capable of. They have no right to do so. And you owe it to yourself to not let them. Yes, some people are more talented than others. But it takes more than talent to succeed.

I remember when the first iPod was released by Apple. I could not afford it. But Campaign Brief Asia, a leading creativity magazine in the region, was giving one away as a gift. You had to fill up the questionnaire and fax back the answer. For three weeks straight, I sent them a fax every day at lunch time. I think they must have been surprised by my persistence. And to my utter surprise, I got a call from them telling me I had won. I remember thinking it was a scam and asked them what I needed to buy. And the woman on the line laughed and said, 'You just need to give me your address and we will courier it over.' And they did. I became a proud iPod winner with 10,000 songs in my pocket.

This is the story of my life. I may not be able to afford something, but when I cannot afford it, I find other ways to attain it, like winning it. Remember my Nokia banana phone which I won at the Nokia Press Night? I also won an $800 Tangs shopping voucher and a few other prizes I wanted. I could barely afford Christmas gifts for my family on my journalist salary, so I had to either make them or win prizes I could re-gift.

Society tells you that there is only one way. The right way. The normal way. But do not forget there is always your own unique way. You just need to find it. Or pave it.

Chapter 5

The Career Woman who Did Not want it All

I gave you a mini glimpse of my career in advertising in the previous chapter. The truth is, when I came to Singapore twenty-one years ago, newly married with my husband and two suitcases, I was not sure what I wanted to do. I tried a bunch of things. Doing an advance Diploma in Creative Arts majoring in vocal performance. Even there, I stuck out like a sore thumb for being different and having an opinion. I have visited and lived temporarily in many countries. But Singapore is the one country that pushes one to a corner to conform in the name of meritocracy.

In all the other countries I had lived in, I struggled to understand the constant changing rules and the idea of what 'good', 'good enough to pass', or 'qualified to get promoted' looked like. This forced me to always shoot for the stars. I believe if you shoot for the stars, you will not end up in the mud. I always pushed to be the best—more specifically, my own definition of 'the best': a better me, beating my own records, pushing my health goals, and I loved aiming for the impossible.

Venturing into the Unknown

In Singapore, however, this was the opposite. Here, meritocracy rules. This can be both good and bad. I realized it even more as

I raise my kids in this country. Here, success is defined through a very thin straw, and one needs to conform and fit into the thin straw and start swimming hard and fast upstream against the tide, towards success. I do not know which is worse, the struggle to find your way and pave your path in an unruly jungle where anything goes, or walking a thin plank and fitting into man-made rules that have a very fixed path to success, except that you have to conform and fit into the mould, and when you reach the end, you realize that while this is one definition of success, you are not sure if it is *your* definition of success.

Which brings me to advertising. I accidentally fell into it. Or rather advertising found me. I had no clue who David Ogilvy was, nor was I acquainted with any of the advertising greats. I had no clue about the construct of the advertising agency, the creative department, and how it functioned. I had no clue what an ad campaign was. And I did not know the name of a single ad agency. That was not the world I was from. That was the world I was taught to think was evil. You know the spiel—advertisements are evil propagandas of corporate folks trying to make money out of you. Advertising folks live in a world of darkness indulging in drunkenness and debauchery. Well, I have to say that there is a lot of drinking. But debauchery and drunkenness? Not any more than any other industry. My favourite thing about ad people? Every bad thing is done in the open, so you know what to expect. And I actually liked the honesty and the openness, the willingness to admit you are doing something bad and do not care to be judged by anyone. I found these people a breath of fresh air. Liberating.

My first year in advertising, I felt guilty about what I was doing. You know, when you are a journalist, you have a voice. You are doing something noble. You are speaking up for the people. When you are in advertising, you are the bitch of the brand. You are being paid to paint a beautiful picture of someone's product. Good or bad, you promote it. You feel like you have sold out.

It did not help that the Christian creative arts school I went to had teachers who shamed folks in advertising, saying that the ad industry was the reason for half the mental problems the world suffered from. There may be some truth in that—advertising does destroy self-esteem by propagating a false standard of beauty which results in low self-image, eating disorders, and such[10]. But ad agencies are not the only problems. I think it is the vicious cycle of governments needing to up their GDP supporting companies wanting to get rich; companies, in turn, hiring ad agencies who want to profit off brands by presenting a false imagery of what is acceptable to or popular in society; young men and women, who want to feel a sense of community and belonging, buying into these lies; and parents and educators, so busy working and trying to feed their families in a world where the one constant is inflation, being forced to compromise family time and values. And these parents and members of the family are the same ones running governments and working for brands and ad agencies.

The advertisements back in the day were mostly created by old, white, sexist men in a society where women were not allowed to speak up, were planted firmly in kitchens, and not consulted in world-changing decisions despite them being the ones with the smarts and ideas on how to make the husband's salary—post gambling and other vices—stretch the whole month, play doctor and medicate the family even when they themselves are sick, ensuring everyone, including the picky eaters, has nutritious food prepared to his or her taste—all this, whilst juggling all other matters of home management; 'management' being the operative word. I always think that if a woman can give birth without throwing in the towel midway (believe me, I was tempted to do that with my

---

[10] Genevieve Morse, 'Women and Advertising—Low Self-Esteem is Good for Profits', *Socialist Alternative*, 2010, https://www.socialistalternative.org/2010/09/05/women-advertising-self-esteem-good-profits/.

first one; story to follow in this chapter) and she has already had
the experience of running her household and pleasing her primary
target audiences of her husband + kids + family pet(s), and juggling
the needs of her secondary target audiences—the extended family,
friends, judgmental neighbours, in-laws—under the tight scrutiny
of her mother in law, she has got all the management experience
needed to run a highly political, intensively volatile corporation.
Now it is a simple matter of repackaging and shifting perspectives.
I tell any woman who has taken a break to have a child, or care for
an ailing parent, that as soon as you are ready to get back to work,
I will help translate your life experience into 'management skills'
that will land you that C-suite job.

One thing I cannot deny about advertising is that you certainly
get paid a lot more than journalism. And despite going in green
and ignorant into a field I was not familiar with, I had a drive
inside of me to thoroughly prepare myself and be competent in
the job I was doing. Perhaps it was just my personality. Perhaps,
it was a manifestation of my ADHD. Whatever it was, I bought
every advertising book I could afford by the old and new ad
greats. I started memorizing good examples of advertisements
and advertising copy. I looked through all the great award-winning
ads and learned how to articulate a big idea. Till now I think this
is a hard one and different people have their own unique ways of
defining and articulating the 'Big Idea'. Ad greats have their own
methodology, and to be honest, some of them contradict each
other. Frankly, it does not matter how you get to it, so long as
you land it. But if you start on your big idea by trying to identify
the problem you want to solve, you have a winner. Unfortunately,
I remember that during my early years in advertising, there was
much time spent coming up with a shiny big idea and very little
time spent understanding the problem we were trying to solve.
And when the big idea does not solve a marketing or business
problem, no matter how shiny it looks, it is useless.

Surviving in a Man's World

Advertising, like journalism, was a man's world. I remember, back at The Star, as I walked into the editorial room, my eyes were assaulted by explicit porn posters and Victoria's Secret calendars on people's tabletops. I have had people literally talk to my boobs or make comments about my baby-bearing hips. At first, I felt embarrassed. Having been a victim of sexual abuse, my self-image was at an all-time low. I was too embarrassed to speak up. Even after what I had experienced, I kept justifying these harassments as a natural extension of the environment I worked in. I told myself, this is what life is like in journalism. Even though I hated it, I kept quiet. I am not proud of that. People say you get used to it, and after a while, you stop hearing it. I never stopped hearing it. It got louder and scratched at my heart harder. And what made me think I had to live with it was the response of the people I worked with, who kept telling me, 'This is how it is in the real world. If you do not get used to it, you can't live in it.' Wrong behaviour is normalized, allowing it to carry on.

A famous American celebrity I had an interview with once grabbed me and made me sit on his lap when I asked to take a picture with him. When my photographer came back to the office, processed the film, and hung it up on the photo room wall, a colleague took it and passed it around. Everyone was exclaiming how lucky I was. I remember smiling at their comment and thinking, 'Why do I not feel lucky? Why do I feel uncomfortable? Is something wrong with me?'

I remember one time I was on an assignment to cover a youth environment story at Fraser Hill in Malaysia. The event was organized by World Wildlife Fund for Nature (WWF) and the media officer was tasked with driving me around and explaining the event, introducing me to people, and arranging for interviews. But he was also harassing me about having a one-night stand. After repeatedly thwarting it off, he drove me to a dark area, which is most of Fraser Hill as it is a nature reserve, and continued pressuring me. He asked me, 'What if a guy like me asked a girl like you to have a one-night stand, what would you do?' And I replied, 'The girl like me would hit the guy like you on the head with this torchlight and run for my life.' He stared straight at me and said, 'Never overestimate your strength, young lady.' I was twenty-three, felt threatened, and became incredibly nervous. I was saved by the sound of wolves howling in the distance. It made him sober up and return me to my accommodation. When I came back home the next day, I went straight to my editor and reported my traumatic encounter. She told me to get used to it, that it comes with the territory of being a female journalist. I remember thinking that this was not okay. I told my colleagues, and funnily, it was the male editors from Intech— the technology pull-out of the Star—who came to my rescue and gave me tips on self-defence. One even kindly handed me a switch blade and told me, 'If anyone tries this on you again, let him get close to you, and when he's least suspecting it, stab it hard into his thigh, twist, and run for your life.' I know violence is not the cure for anything, but self-defence is. And these guys asked me if I needed them to teach the WWF media officer a lesson he would not forget. No one hurt anyone, but the fact that they thought I was treated wrongly and should have been protected made me feel so much better than the reaction of my editor. What she said made me question myself and my rights as female journalist. It made me wonder if I was doing something wrong that made me a magnet for perverts. I knew what was happening to me was wrong, but I did not have the guidance, the know-how nor the avenue to make it right. There was no information, no access to Google or the internet. And I was living in a society where people would normally brush off my complaints and ask me questions like, 'What were you wearing to make him come onto you?' 'Why were you alone in the dark with him?'

The reaction of these people was enforcing the false notion that as long as you are female, expect to get hit on by men. And when men hit on you, it is usually because of how you present yourself or what you wear. And the only way to protect yourself from one man is by getting another man to rescue you and teach that wayward man—who cannot help himself because he is male, not to mention you encouraged him—a lesson by beating him up. There were no lessons on how women were to help themselves, stand up for themselves, protect themselves. You had to go and ask another man to protect you. Why? More often than not, there was no man around to rescue me. I was left to my own wit and devices to defend myself and get through an uncomfortable situation.

The same was true of advertising. You really must be smarter, sharper, and better as a woman to stand up and be counted. I mentioned earlier in the book that I had won awards in my first year in advertising. It made me think to myself, 'Hey I am good at this. This is my god-given gift. I am not going to let anyone take this away from me.' And so, I let the guilt slide off my newly coated Teflon-skin and embraced it.

Both journalism and copywriting are jobs where you must be a skilled writer. Both require you to tell stories albeit for different purposes in different styles, but the result is the same. And yet the perception of the religious community is that one is more noble than the other. After a year of crossing over to advertising, I finally came to terms with my newfound role. I loved the creativity and coming up with ideas. I was born to do this. I was in a profession I loved and was thriving at it. I started feeling good and joyful about my occupation and started owning it. During that time, I would occasionally join my granduncle Bill, a missionary, on trips to rural India.

The village missions pastor used to introduce me with so much pride and respect when I was a journalist—'Here is *Sister* Uma, a journalist from Singapore . . .' And when I joined the ad world and told them, I was awaiting an equally illustrious introduction, but all I got was a pathetic, 'Here is *Sister* Uma, she used to be a journalist,' and it stopped there.

I learned some of my best lessons in life from working in advertising. It was a job I was not sure about, then fell madly in love with. I loved how folks in advertising were open about their shortcomings, exhibited their emotional outburst without restraint, and in doing so, created a safe environment that allowed me to be me.

But advertising in Singapore, as in most parts of the world, was very much an old white man's domain. When I joined the ad world, I was not ambitious. I was not apologetic either. I just did my best and celebrated the victory that resulted from it. I did not do it for more increments or promotions. It was just in my DNA to want to be the best at what I do.

Making the Choice to Choose Me for a Change

During that time, my husband and I were also trying to start a family and have a baby. After seven hard years of trying to have a baby, when I finally got pregnant, I suffered a miscarriage. I blamed myself. I was heartbroken. I could barely get out of bed. I felt like God had played a nasty trick on me and pulled the rug out from underneath my feet. I started questioning how many bad things a single human being can endure.

I am generally a very optimistic person. Yes, I tried to take my life twice, but I got out of it. I took the fact that I escaped the clutches of my godfather without dying as a second chance at life. My dad, the person I loved most on the planet died young of cancer, and as a result, I suffered from six whole months of insomnia, but I overcame that too. I never gave up trying to have a baby. Throughout all the bad things that happened to me,

I did my best to never give up on life and destiny. But when I lost my baby, it really knocked the wind off my sail. I was empty. And it did not help that people close to me blamed me for what had happened, stating I did not take care of the baby in my womb and that was why I lost it. I had a handful of good friends who texted me every day and encouraged me. That meant a lot and gave me the daily dose of energy to get out of bed.

Every year on my birthday (because I was getting a year older and the chances of getting pregnant were getting slimmer) and Christmas (because God gave a virgin a Son, and here I was begging for one), I would look to heaven, weep, lament, and literally yell at God about how unfair it was that he would shut my womb and not give me a child. How had he put me through so much and continue to ill-treat me? Where was the justice in this?

Finding the Will to Be Strong at my Weakest Moment

I remember the day I did my pregnancy test and realized I was pregnant. I was in a daze. I could not believe it. My husband took extra care of me, thinking I was going to break. I decided that now that I had the baby in me, nothing could take it away. It was a sealed deal. I felt it was a boy. And I went through the days so hopeful, with so much joy. Little did I know that that joy would be short-lived.

We would visit the gynae biweekly at the National University Hospital (NUH) to have my scan done to see the baby's growth and heartbeat. That tiny little blinking light of a heartbeat on the screen gave me so much joy. I read the Bible and Pablo Neruda to the baby every night.

Then, that one day when Colin could not accompany me, when I thought it was just another visit to see the same thing, it was anything but. There was no blinking light, which meant there was no beating heart. I felt as if someone had put out the lamp in my heart. I had to sit through it alone. No one to hold my hand. My gynae looked at me with so much sadness, I knew all hope was lost.

But I asked for one month to come back and test again. Every day I prayed over my baby for life to be restored. It was a stressful month with me willing my child to live. And when I went back, there was still no heartbeat. At twelve weeks, the foetus had shrunk a bit. That was when a dilation and curettage (D&C) was ordered. It is a procedure to remove the remaining foetal tissue from inside the uterus. I had to have whatever was left of my baby surgically removed. I remembered laying in the room waiting to be wheeled-in to the operating theatre, feeling cold inside. And then I thought of my dad in heaven, welcoming his little grandson, and I told myself it will all be all right.

It took months before I was emotionally all right.

And after two years, I got pregnant again. Now, this pregnancy was strange. I remember waking up one morning in December 2007, feeling I was going to be pregnant soon—that very month. I called my mom and informed her of my intuition and asked her to pray. My friend in my acapella group dreamed we were on a tour, and I was pregnant. I was playing one of the lead characters in a musical. My acapella group had just launched our album, and we were doing back-to-back album launch tours. It was the busiest season of our lives, and yet I knew this was the month I would conceive. I told my husband. God bless that man; he believes everything I tell him, no matter how cuckoo it sounds, which is what I love about him. Even when I doubt myself, he has absolute faith in me and encourages me to do the impossible.

Society tells you a woman needs to be a mother to be whole. But I realized my body could only prepare itself to be what it was meant to be when I set myself free from societal expectation and told myself I wanted to be a mother for myself, not to fit into someone else's definition of a married woman.

I believed despite the years it took that I was meant to be a mom. I was called to be a mom. And the second I realized that, everything inside me aligned and I was ready to be a mom. A spotted zebra can only achieve its full potential when it knows that what it wants is for itself, and not to please someone else.

By January, I found out I was pregnant. I had to get these nasty, extremely expensive weekly jabs on my bottom the first trimester to support my pregnancy. And the jabs gave me such bad mood swings, I had to centre myself every day, speak positive words over my life, and channel good feelings towards my child. I did not want a depressed, grumpy child. I did yoga and swam ten laps every night. But I had the worst nightmares throughout my pregnancy about demons coming to steal my child. I fought my dreams and chose to stay positive in my waking hours. I was careful about the words I used. I did my best to fill my home with only good vibes and positive emotions despite feeling crappy inside. The fear that I could lose this baby was too real.

With prayer, sheer willpower, and positivity, I went through the pregnancy. The second I found out I was pregnant, I quit my job. I was putting in long hours and I did not think this would be conducive to my health or my pregnancy.

Finding Kindness in an Unkind Environment

Then I found out that the agency I worked at had lost a key account and there would be retrenchments. I was group head of copy. And I was lucky because my very decent and very humane boss tore up my resignation letter and gave me a severance package instead because I was working on the key brand.

Whatever you may say about advertising being a harsh and cruel environment, there were many unique moments like these where I tasted compassion and kindness. It reminded me there were good people to be found everywhere. It also reminded me to keep it real in an environment known to be 'plastic'. While it may be hard to seek out and build lasting relationships while everyone is expecting you to have your screensaver up and guard your heart, it is okay to let your guard down and be your authentic self. I learned that there were many times when people took advantage of my genuineness and transparency. Yes, they hurt me. But there were also many times when I saw goodness and kindness, and these moments made it worth it.

I still freelanced when I was pregnant. We could not afford to live in Singapore with a baby on the way on a single salary. But that has always been the thing I was taught. When I talk to my peers and fellow Singaporeans, most believe in saving up, gathering enough, training themselves up, getting all the information before taking a leap of faith. I took the step and trusted that I can find creative ways to provide for myself.

The reality is if you behave like everyone else, you will be holding yourself back. Having had very little in my early years, I learned from watching my parents to always reach for more, to take a leap of faith. Even when I do not have enough, if I really want something, I will just get it and figure out how to pay for it later. I have too much honour to ask for money or get someone to buy it for me. But I know once I set my mind and sight on something, and I buy it, I always find a way to earn the money I need to pay for it. Because as I have mentioned in previous chapters, money is merely the means, the end is the thing that brings me joy.

Generosity is a Choice, Not an Outcome

People also think generosity is giving from your abundance. My parents showed me that generosity is not the result of the state of your bank account. That is what most people believe. You give your leftovers, or you give for tax deduction purposes that end up ultimately benefiting you. My parents taught me to always have an abundance mindset. To give even when I do not have enough. In university, I paid for two students' fees. I did it with money I earned. I could have kept that money for myself, to buy and own nice things. Ironically, the thought of spending money on myself did not even cross my mind. Having watched the generosity and kindness of my parents, whenever I get extra money, I always think about who I can help support and grow. My husband used to complain that I would give things away, but when people are in need, I have not met anyone more generous than him. It has been the same with my creative teams. When the pitch budget does not allow for it, I would buy pizza and dinner for the team with my own money to appreciate and celebrate them for staying late. Birthday cakes, cards, and team presents all came out of my pocket because I believe in sowing into people's lives and blessing them not because I have extra, but because I choose to share what I have, and this brings me great joy.

Now I am so grateful for that mindset because while it goes against the norm, it really is the best investor mindset. Most people invest in the stock market by studying the ups and downs of the market movement. From the moment I could afford to, I put my money in brands I believed in because whether they sink or soar, at least I know I have put my money where my heart is.

I went with the same attitude when I freelanced. I was tired of being told women would make bad creative directors, that women are not suited to work as advertising creatives, and that women have their period every month and do not show up to work. Irrespective of how horrible I felt, I went in every morning into the ad agency on time, finished my work and left. I was told on my second week freelancing that in the last month, six copywriters had been fired. I lasted the whole nine months. I was given freelance projects to do from home during my maternity leave. And my daily freelance rate had increased by close to 40 per cent and they begged me to come back and work after I had my baby. I remember my husband proudly telling everyone what an independent entrepreneurial spirit I have, and that nothing can get in my way.

Here Comes the Baby

Having a baby was not a bed of roses. There were challenges. The baby was due on 28 September, but I went into labour at 4 a.m. on September 24, my birthday. If you have never expected a baby, here is something you should know. In your final month, as the baby gets bigger and fills up a lot of the space in your belly, you start counting kicks, there is a minimal number of kicks daily to tell you all is well with baby.

On 23 September, the baby hardly kicked, and I got very nervous. After waiting all evening and getting less than ten kicks, I told my husband that there was something wrong with the baby, we should go to the hospital. I was especially nervous because a few weeks prior we had moved house. Yes, just my hubby and I packing up things and moving them. I ended up having rashes on my thigh from sweat and the weight of pregnancy and had to see the gynae to get meds. I was afraid that all of that had affected the baby. When I showed up at the hospital, they ran a scan. I was told the baby was fine, but I was three cm dilated. For the uninitiated, one's cervix must be 100 per cent effaced and ten cm dilated before a vaginal delivery. Then, they asked if I would like to get admitted.

Having spent a lot of time reading up on giving birth and raising a baby on Google, I had read that a person can be three cm dilated a whole week. I learned later that this was not necessarily true for all. When in doubt, ask the medical experts rather than Google. On that day, I decided to go home and straight to bed. At 4 a.m., I went into labour. I felt these sharp pains increase in intensity. They became more and more frequent, and I took out my stopwatch to time it. I woke my husband up and told him, 'Do not panic, but I think the baby is on its way.'

After an episode of Googling to ensure I was going into labour, and an attempt to shave my legs so that I did not look like a yeti while giving birth, we finally left our home in the east to get to the hospital in the west of Singapore. The roads were clear as we made our way to NUH. Going into labour at 4 a.m. and not during peak hours was a blessing because during the Formula One season, the roads were usually blocked, closed, or full of traffic.

I was nervous and excited at the same time. And then, everything that could go wrong went wrong. It took 45 minutes and 6 misses before the anaesthetist got the epidural in. I do not know how I held still for that long but by the time he had finished, there was a puddle of blood behind me. Midway through to delivery, the epidural malfunctioned and dripped on my back. I had to carry on through the rest of the labour without painkillers. The doctors could not detect my baby's heartbeat at one point, so they had to attach a stent to his head to monitor the vitals. I was ten cm dilated and the baby's head was not crowned. They had to give me oxytocin to speed up the labour. The midwife started discussing the possibility of a C-section. And I looked her in the eye and growled, 'No! Not after what I had gone through. Misses on the epidural. Failed epidural. I am going to push this baby out.' And so, with absolute focus and all my muscles, I pushed the baby till his head was crowned. And then my gynae was called just in time to catch Daniel and welcome him into the world. This torturous delivery was followed by twenty-nine excruciating stitches without painkiller.

When the gynae passed me Daniel, I had barely enough energy to check him and ensure all his essential body parts— finger, toes, and privates included—were intact before passing out of sheer exhaustion. I remember having a fever, thanks to all the pain I bore.

No one prepares you for having a baby. I remember giving birth out of sheer determination, without any painkillers, because I had to get this baby out, healthy and well. I did not have a choice. I did not have the option to throw in the towel and say this is it, I cannot do it. I quit. Let us stuff the baby back up. I am going home to watch TV. The irony is organizations see a woman who takes time off to have a baby as weak. They paint her as a woman retreating to take care of her family and spending time at home. It is seen as a passive, docile thing. But, in fact, it is the opposite. A woman giving birth is like a man going into battle.

Your body is torn and broken when you give birth. You change, nurture, and nurse your child while you yourself are recovering from having something taken out of you, stitched up, suffering from blood and iron loss, massive hormonal changes, lack of sleep and a constant feeling of inadequacy and weakness. You see, it is the first time you have been given a child to handle. And even if it is your second, every child is different. The emotional and mental weight of wanting to do the right thing by that child weighs heavily on you. Unlike running a business where finances get screwed up if you fail, here a life could get harmed.

You are fighting against your body and letting your love and willpower prevail to stay focused and plan your time around this new, erratic, surprising life. You have so many mixed emotions—joy, love, and then there is absolute turmoil, fear, doubt, and anger. All this in the first four to six months of having a baby. Do not get me wrong, after nine years of desperately wanting a child and a miscarriage, I was elated at the thought of having a baby. But as I mentioned earlier, I also have ADHD and it means my emotions and logic are clearly separated. By the time the feeling of being overwhelmed caught up, I had long completed the task. Being a world-class 'compartmentalizer', I struggled extra hard to work around a baby who did not give two hoots for my plans. He had his own idea of how the hours should be spent and made sure I knew about it.

Letting Go and Going with the Flow

And that is another thing that goes against societal norms. During the first three months of raising Daniel, I struggled. I was trying to teach my child to follow my schedule—sleep when I slept, wake up when I had enough rest, drink when I wanted him to drink so he can finish on time for me to get work done or catch my favourite TV series. Nope, he wanted to do his own thing and show me he was boss of his time and mine. Losing control was hard emotionally, mentally, and physically. I was exhausted and perturbed. I felt I was to blame for his lack of discipline and my incompetence.

Then I spoke to my mom, who had raised four kids without any help, and she gave me the best advice ever. 'Throw away the self-help parenting books. You have everything within you to raise this child. This child is yours. And he has no clue when you are screwing things up, he has no other moms to compare you to, he's not grading you on your performance. Forget about the schedules. Just go with the flow.'

Go with the flow? She might as well have told me to leave the child at the door of an orphanage with a 'Please take care of my baby' note and run away. Well, long story short, I took her advice with great reluctance, fear, and trepidation and allowed myself to fail as a parent.

And then I realized my baby behaved better. He was calmer when I became more relaxed about my parenting. My husband heaved a clear sigh of relief now that I was not throwing tantrums and having panic fits while bossing him about. The man was a saint, patiently putting up with his nightmare of a wife.

And this is the spotted zebra lesson I learned. We are taught to plan. You know that famous Benjamin Franklin quote, 'When you fail to plan, you are planning to fail.' The truth is, sometimes, we cannot plan everything. I learned to accept that and understand that sometimes you must simply stop planning and go with the flow. It may not lead you to success as the world sees it, but it will definitely take you down the path of joy, surprises, and a better mental state.

Another thing society holds you hostage to—you are not allowed to make spontaneous decisions without having all the facts in front of you. But the truth is, there is never a point in your life where you will ever have all the facts you need to make the right decision. Here is another spotted zebra lesson: do the best you can with what you know, and that is enough to enjoy the best life with the people around you and the time you have.

Giving up All to Raise a Kind Child

Daniel was a child with great compassion. I could see this from the time he was young. He was just naturally kind to other kids. And no matter how mean they were, he never retaliated. I was stunned by this natural inclination towards good. It made me more maternal. In some ways, having a baby helped my sense of emotion and logic align a little closer.

Daniel would never tell on a kid who got him into trouble because he could not bring himself to hurt another kid. He would go in early to class and arrange the other kids' desks for them while they were out at recess, so that when the Neatness Nazi of a Chinese teacher came into class, she would not yell at the kids. She was the one who noticed what Daniel was doing and told me about it. During a parent teacher meeting, she informed me how poorly Daniel was doing in Chinese but how well he was doing as a human being and child. 'He is excelling in life,' she said to me.

'He's the kindest and sweetest boy I know, and if I could give him an A for that, I would.' It made me cry. It was one of the best things a teacher had said to me about my son—that he was turning into a wonderful human being. That is more important to me than his grades.

I took Daniel to work often when I had to stay back, just so he would be in a creative environment and understand what mommy was doing. I wanted him to see how much I enjoyed my work and how he needs to find something he loves and do it, that work was not a chore or something you did just to earn money. Of course, in the early days, my helper came along. She seemed to love being in an ad agency as well. But as the kids grew older, they wanted to follow me to work on their own, make their own friends in the office, and participate in the creative process. I loved the independence and passion. It allowed my kids to be around me, and I also knew they were safe. They felt mom was in the same 'house' as them. And work to them was not work. It was an after-school activity. They joined my colleagues for lunch and had conversations about campaigns and ideas. It was good for them and great for me.

A Fresh Take on Ambition

I was not ambitious when I had Daniel. Well, at least not in the way I am today. I literally took a step back from building my career and pushed to build up my son into a good human. I wanted the opposite of what society wanted. In Singapore, when I have conversations with parents, it is all around the corporate pressure of trying to succeed within that thin straw of meritocracy I talked about earlier. I did not fit in. And I did not want to shape my child to fit into it. I wanted to raise a member of the human race, not someone who fit into a socio-political, cultural mould defined by one system.

If aliens visited the earth and asked for a sample of humanity's best, what would this look like? It would not be the one person or one group of people looking the same. It would be a group of people with different strengths, individually unique, misfits even, but as a collective functioning as one by complementing each other and beautifully representing the human race. And I want to raise a son who would fit into this group, not simply meet a very prescriptive societal expectation.

There is so much emphasis on being happy today. But really, happiness is not something you arrive at one day because you have quit your job, run off to a beach, and decided to eat, pray, love. It is a journey that we are on where, at each crossroad and path, we need to make choices that would fill up our cup of joy a bit more. We need to choose joy in our daily interactions. The spotted zebra sees happiness as a mindset. And I wanted to build that mindset in my son. But beyond happiness, I wanted him to understand the value of satisfaction. And that can only come from finding your purpose and living it out.

There is the fake notion of an ambition—becoming something when you grow up. Thanks to Google and exposure to the internet, today's kids know that there are a lot more opportunities in the world, more things they could be outside of the standard doctor, lawyer, accountant, and engineer. But we still ask them, what do you want to be when you grow up as if:

a) They cannot be what they want to be immediately now. Why not? Why are we stopping them? My daughter, Sarah, said she wants to run a café at the tender age of nine. I got permission from the condo management and got her to do a mini bake sale near the kid's pool. She made everything, sold it cheap, and people bought it. They wanted more, so it became a weekend thing. Covid happened. It ended. But now, after all that practice, she caters goodie bags with baked stuff for people's events.

b) An occupation is what every child should aspire towards, making it seem once again like what you make of yourself and how much money you earn doing it is the end objective.

I really wanted the opposite for my son. I wanted him to know that he does not have to wait till he grows up to explore the things he loves, or go to university to study the things he wants. He needs to be whatever he can be now. And take whatever courses he wants to learn today. Society says you need to wait till you are the right age to pick up something new. And then, they say, you are too old to do other things.

There is always an age label placed on people. But the spotted zebra is ageless and is never too young nor too old to learn something new, to try something different. I am constantly challenging him to think about what he enjoys doing, what he is passionate or curious about, then think how he can find out more about it and learn it. He does not have to wait till he goes to school or graduates from university to do the things he loves and start earning money doing it. The entrepreneurial spirit is without age limitations.

I also wanted him to know he can change his mind anytime. I would rather he explored and learned many different things than stick to the one thing for years on end, even if he grows to dread it. Schools, education systems, and parents tell kids to stick to the one thing and master it, but what is the point if along the way they find a new passion, discover they are not good at this thing, or find something they are better at? They should be allowed to pursue it. While he may have had a foundation in physics, Elon Musk decided to study rocket science late in life because he wanted to build rockets that could land vertically and be reused, and everyone told him it is impossible. Learning should be lifelong. This means, at any point you should be allowed to pick up a new skill.

The second thing I wanted to teach my son, which is against the new woke culture, is that opposing opinions are good. You do not have to agree with everything someone says. You need to hold on to your own truth with conviction. But you must also listen to someone else's truth as long as it does not go against human rights and harm living things, even if you vehemently disagree. Always look at a situation from different perspectives; you do not have to accept, nor agree, or give in to someone else's perspective. But you owe it to yourself to keep an open mind because you never know which truth you might borrow, adapt, or convert to as you grow in life. The truth you hold on to today may change tomorrow as you grow. But if you have no exposure to new truths and different perspective, you are stuck under your rock and cannot grow. You cannot change. You cannot evolve and be better. Therefore, a change of government, leaders, and fresh blood are important in politics and in organizations. People are afraid of change. They always say that if it is not broken, why fix it? Yes, we can go with what works, but after a while, it becomes mundane, boring, safe, and there is no progress. Sometimes, the old way needs to be broken to make space for something new and better.

And here is the most important thing I wanted to teach my son, the best lesson for little spotted zebra babies. Nothing good is easy. Nothing worthwhile is effortless. If something scares you, face your fears and do it. You might fail. But it is your failure. You did it trying something new. And you own it. It is better than not trying because society, your parents (yes, his father and I), your teachers told you it is not safe, do not do it, no one has done it before. Peter Thiel, a German-American billionaire entrepreneur, venture capitalist, political activist, and co-founder of PayPal says something along the lines of how society always tells you that if it is something worth doing, something new, novel, and money making, surely someone else would have done it by now. Well, maybe you are the one who is meant to do it. Maybe no one has thought of it. You will never know until and unless you take that leap of faith and do it.

I also told my son, 'If you really believe something is right and worth doing, do it. I may think the opposite and punish you for doing it. But if it is worth it and means that much to you, do it anyway, then accept the punishment, pay the price, get grounded.'

I remember there was a period when my son would tell me, 'Mom, I feel stressed, I feel like quitting.' I always talk through his emotions with him. I help him evaluate his stress level and talk to him about it. But I also know deep inside every human being is this raging battle. The excellent spirit: the need to push ourselves, to do more, to achieve what we were meant to do. It fights against complacency, the other side inside you telling you to take it easy. There is a need to balance this. Today society is saying the opposite. Take it easy. Do not over-exert and end up with mental health issues.

We need to be careful to balance this. Every child, actually, every human being, needs someone to talk to, to understand your limits, to know when you are overstraining and when to push hard. I have ADHD, so limits do not exist. My mom figured this out early and set strict rules to make me stop working. My husband starts nagging me when he thinks I am working myself to death. I have no clue I am doing this. My friends joke that if there is a task to be done, even if I lose a leg and arm in the process, I will still push and complete the task, ahead of everyone else. I used to think this was a complement, but now that I have kids, I consciously ask the people I love to stop me when they see triggers that show I am pushing too hard. I am glad I have people I feel safe with, whom I know love me, and can honestly knock me into seeing that I am working myself way past healthy limits.

With my son, I do not want him to give into the part that is lazy or tells him to take a step back when his potential is so much more. And I am not talking about studies, I am talking about all the things he loves, and who he is. We had this talk a few times, where I explained how this inner battle works and told him if he pushes himself, if he pays the price and puts in the effort, when he learns something new, masters a new skill, or succeeds at something he set out to do, he will be satisfied when he lies in bed at night, knowing he gave his best that day. Whether it succeeded or failed is not the point. The point is he knows deep inside he gave his best shot and he is proud of himself.

He sat with me thinking it through. And now it has become a practice for him. So much so that when I walk in and ask him to take it easy, remind him he does not have to be great at everything he does, talk to him about prioritizing, he turns around and tells me, 'Mom, I signed up for these things. I need to feel that I gave it my best shot. That I tried, mom. If I get too tired, I'll stop.' While it breaks my heart to see him exhausted at times or feeling sad when he fails at something he has been trying so hard to accomplish, it gives me great pride that he is doing his best to live his life to the fullest.

It is the exact same thing I tell my creative team. Having a son gave me a lot of insights into mentoring young men and women to be their best selves. Many times, I have sat with my team and managed them by remembering how I dealt with my son. What would I want for him? How would I want him to grow up? And I try and do the same for these young ones who are entering the world of advertising, whom I am mentoring. I also believe strongly in paying in advance—that as I guide these young ones to the best of my ability, wanting them to succeed and get far in life, one day, someone else will do the same for my kids.

Society sets rules for our children to fit into a fixed mould to do well in life by their standards. We need to break that mould to see what shape and form our children take. Most times, this shape changes as they grow. We need to allow that growth to see them become their own beautiful versions of themselves and not just conform to the vision of them that we or society have. Some people see life as an uphill drive to their goals. When I had my son, I realized my life took an up, down, curvy, and roundabout path.

The lesson from the spotted zebra here is that it is not about goals. It is about living by your own values, things that fill you with love, joy, and peace. You do not have to compete with others to get to the top of the hill. You must find what matters to you. What does success mean to you? What is it you value? It does not matter if others look down on those values or judge you for it. We often compare ourselves and our families against the wrong things, all the things that do not matter. What matters is your joy and happiness, and that sense of fulfilment.

When I quit my job and went into freelancing, as a brown, Asian woman, I was practically pulling the breaks on my career. People could not understand why I was going to give up an uphill career to have a baby. Only I did. When I went back to advertising, I had to start from scratch. I was not afraid of it. Frankly, I should not have had to. But at that time, I was willing to. The price I paid was worth it. My son was better for it. And I had a greater sense of fulfilment than a big title would have gotten me.

Chapter 6

The Daughter Who Sent Me to War

'When you're on someone else's field, you have to play by their rules,' the principal of a music school I once attended told me. He was basically asking me to toe the line. I turned around and told him with as much fierceness I could muster, 'No matter whose field I am on, I play by the principles that I hold true—to do the right thing every chance I get.'

Finding Courage to Change the Rules

I live by my own rules and the voice of my conscience. When you have children, you need to do this even more. When I had a son, I learned to be more mature and nurturing. My lens had a maternal filter. When I had a daughter, my lens took on a warrior filter. It was not planned. It just happened naturally.

After having a son, we got brave and decided to try for a second child for a slew of different reasons. I was not getting any younger. We did not want our son to be alone. We both had siblings, and, as annoying as they are, they also contributed in a big way to who we became. It is nice to have someone else to play with, fight with, and channel the focus on during family get-togethers and when annoying relatives are present.

We decided to try without any help from the gynae this time. I was the associate creative director at a big multinational corporation, and I was incredibly busy working on a global skincare account. We tried and nothing happened. I got really busy at work. I suggested to my husband that we put it off as this might not be the best time to bring a baby into the world. I was so stressed out after client meetings, I started throwing up. That was when a close colleague pointed out, 'You're throwing up an awful lot. You sure you're not preggers?' The thought caught me by surprise. No way, I would know if I was. So, that day during lunch, at the ION Orchard Food Court toilet, I did a pregnancy test. And to my surprise, I was pregnant.

I remember sitting down at the table, staring at my half-eaten lunch while dialling my husband's number. I was excited and exhausted, all at the same time. It all felt surreal. With Daniel, getting pregnant was such an effort. With Sarah, just when I decided to give up, she showed up. Like summer snow, an unexpected sign that I am going to be doubly blessed. I prayed for a child. I was blessed with two—a son *and* a daughter. The nine years of waiting was well worth it.

The pregnancy with Sarah was much easier emotionally but exhausting physically. I had a fulltime job at JWT Singapore. I was putting in long hours. I had an active, demanding toddler I had to look after, and I was worried about how he would take to his mommy having another baby.

I was struggling with the dumbest things. Can I love another child as much as I love this one? Will this child feel unloved because there is a second child in the home? Honestly, a lot of these thoughts were not even my own. They came from books I was reading on parenting, setting imaginary parameters that suddenly started limiting me and my capacity to parent. The books, a wide number of them with opposing opinions, were seeding negative thoughts that were not there to begin with. It was only much later that I realized that every child is unique, every parent has a unique way of raising their child. You need to find what works for you and your child. No one can write a book to define the chemistry and relationship you are going to have with your child. That is yours to own. Own it and work with it. Only after realizing this was I able to release the guilt, shame, and doubts about parenting and be the best parent I can be.

Remember I said that I used to shout in the direction of heaven every birthday and Christmas, 'God, where is my baby?' Well, Daniel was born on my birthday. And Sarah was due on Christmas. I prayed hard that she would come early. No baby deserves to get one combined present for both Christmas and her birthday. As you can tell, I have some very strange life priorities. Sarah was born on 22 December 2010. Once again, I went into labour at 4 a.m. I woke my husband gently and told him, 'Moo Moo (term of endearment, do not judge), my water broke.' He woke up in a fright and asked me who broke it. I calmly told him, 'My water broke. I am going into labour. Can you get me a towel?' Then I called the labour ward to tell them I was coming in. And I had shaved my legs well in advance, so I was all set to go and give birth with confidence this time.

It was the easiest labour. The night before, my husband had to perform with my acapella group at Sentosa. I was part of the group but took a break due to the pregnancy. When he came home, Daniel was in his diaper on the dining table, assisting me with apple strudels. I do not know if it was because of all the baking I had done while she was in my womb, but my daughter is an amazing baker. She can bake croissants, croquembouches, and all sorts of fancy things from scratch. And she hopes to become a baker one day, giving Adriano Zumbo and Gordon Ramsay, her two idols, a run for their money. Her dream is to quit school (she is in grade 6) and join the Cordon Bleu. And believe me, she has the capability, skill, and mettle to hold her own amongst any professional chef twice her age. In fact, at her young age, she is already catering for events and book launches and earning her keep. A big part of the funds goes to #TeamSeas—her favourite charity run by the famous YouTubers, MrBeast and Mark Robber—to clean up the ocean.

All those years of taking my kids to the ad agency while I was busy, have not been wasted. They can create their own concept boards, come up with big ideas, and sell their ideas for money. They even ask me to help them draft indemnity forms when they sell things to their classmates to ensure there are no liabilities and that they do not get into trouble. It is crazy how much they pick up from observing and trying versus sitting down in a classroom and learning from a textbook. Contextual learning is so much more powerful than classroom education. That is one of the most powerful lessons I have learned from having kids. In fact, I learned how to learn by watching them learn. Here is a great spotted zebra lesson—you do not just educate those in your care, you also learn from them.

From the second I walked in, the nurses started laughing and said I was the happiest and most relaxed mom-to-be they had seen. With Sarah, giving birth was a walk in the park. It took ten minutes to insert the epidural. It worked like a charm, and in between pushes, I even discussed the apple strudel recipe with my gynae. Sarah had the sweetest smile when she was born. And the first thing I did was breastfeed her. She was the opposite of Daniel. While he drank away voraciously, she fell asleep the second her cheeks touched my breast. She was just as difficult to breastfeed for a whole different reason. After multiple visits to the midwives for help on how to breastfeed, I gave up and decided to pump and feed her. Being unable to breastfeed her was another dent on my confidence as a mother, a shadow on my mothering ability. Society has a way of defining you by certain characteristics to add shame to the already colossal task of parenting. I wanted to feed my child breastmilk because it was good for her and boosted her immunity. It was my mom of all people who pointed out, 'What does it matter whether you feed her directly or pump it out and give it to her in the bottle? Do not beat yourself up. Your child is still drinking your milk.'

We set such ridiculously high bars for ourselves when we turn the means into the end. Breastfeeding was not the end result. Ensuring my child got breastmilk was the end result I was after.

Facing a Whirlwind of Change

Then came the big challenge. After four months of maternity leave, I had to return to ad land. I had to pump milk in an agency that failed to consider breastfeeding moms in the design of its new office where all the rooms had glass walls. I was reduced to pumping milk—that is, preparing my newborn's meal—in a toilet cubicle, sometimes with someone making poop on my right. I would go in with a basket full of cleaning supplies just to ensure the cubicle I was using was clean and well disinfected. There is just no way of playing this down. It was gross. It was obvious that men planned the layout of this office. That is why you need both men and women to be involved in UX and design, thinking for everything. One cannot think for the other. You need to describe what life is like walking in someone else's shoes and ensure that both genders' journeys are accounted for.

I cannot tell you how many times I have gone into that toilet, pumped milk and cried thinking that this was what I am feeding Sarah. With Daniel, I was still freelancing, and I got to do it in the comfort of my home. With Sarah at JWT, it felt criminal to have to pump milk for my baby in such a degrading environment. And then to squeeze the pack of pumped milk in a freezer full of other disgusting things that people failed to empty for months. Just thinking about it makes me sick to the stomach.

Like I said in the title of this chapter, my daughter sent me to war. You know, those same sexual innuendos I tolerated or considered part of being a woman in ad land, they became completely unbearable after I had a daughter. The lack of consideration for women in general, and the notion of 'Oh, poor you, you're going to have your period every month, or go off and have a baby, or take four months on maternity, so I need to think twice about hiring you or promoting you.' I wasn't going to take it sitting down.

Now, do not get me wrong. I do not think women are better than men. I have a wonderful husband, an amazing son, and was raised by the best father in the world. I have had some shitty men in my life, but the ones close to me were mostly amazing. And they always made me feel like I could do the impossible. But in the workplaces I have been in, the notion that men are more capable than women, they deserve to be promoted faster and paid more than women, and they should be allowed to make derogatory and sexually inappropriate remarks about women was not something I was going to take sitting down. Prior to having a daughter, I chose to let it slide off my Teflon skin, thinking and hoping someone else would set it right, waiting for the organizations to wake up and do the right thing, for some advertising body to set rules that protected women in the workplace. There was also so much more at stake. All those sexually inappropriate remarks were not a lack of education or people behaving badly. It was people in authority and power lording it over those under them. It was a sick way of controlling those under you. And because of this, most women said nothing, fearing for their jobs, and the fact that their work environment would be miserable if they said anything.

Once I had my daughter, I decided to be the change I wanted to see. And what triggered it was just imagining my daughter in each of those situations, on the receiving end. Society tells us when we see something wrong and it does not affect us directly, we are to mind our own business, to keep our heads down and walk away. Why make someone else's problem your own?

A spotted zebra knows that when you see something wrong and do nothing about it, you are partially responsible for the problem. You are to blame. You are a passive contributor to the normalization of a wrongdoing. Evil rises in the world because everyone who bore witness to it went along with it or pretended not to see it. When we hear violent, abusive domestic squabbles in our neighbourhood, how many of us dare to knock on the door and check what is happening or call the security guards or the cops? I would. Because that could be me or someone I love crying for help. And contrary to what people believe, you do not need to make dramatic gestures or go on a rampage to bring about change. A butterfly effect can occur, and change can be set in motion by simply speaking up politely when you see something wrong.

When I was the global creative director at a large American ad agency, I heard from two male expat colleagues that their children were covered by the company insurance. When I spoke to HR about it, I was told they are men, and the Singapore law does not cover kids of female employees. Now, for an American agency that takes pride in equality and treating their employees fairly, this was unacceptable. I did not care what the law stated. I cared about what was right. So, I kept writing emails and letters to different people in the organization. Yes, I got a lot of run around. But I was polite and persistent, stating my case till my insurance got adjusted to cover my kids. I could have kept this to myself like they asked me to. But I said I would not. If the male staff were getting their kids covered under the insurance, then every female employee deserved the same. And it started a slow but sure chain reaction where HR was forced to look at the benefits accorded to female staff against male staff in the agency.

In this advertising agency, I was also the only female global creative director for the many years I worked there. I also hired and contributed to the hiring of two of the five female creatives in the main agency. I remember being asked if I did it because they were women. I hired them because they were just as capable or in some cases better than the men who applied, and I wanted to put my money where my mouth was and balance out the status quo and hire more women in a mostly male dominated creative department.

Once a month, the creative directors would meet with the Chief Creative Office (CCO) at my agency to discuss work in progress and awards ideas. We would gather in the board room in the creative department. The first time I attended this meeting, I realized, I was the only female. I was tempted to take the back seat or stand in a corner. There were not enough seats to go around, and this was what some did. And as the newbie, I guess, there was some unspoken rule that I do just that. Amid all these men, I did not feel I belonged. Then I thought of the Chief Operating Officer of Facebook, Sheryl Sandberg's words to lean in and take my seat at the table[11]. And I thought of my daughter, what I would want her to do. And so, I looked at where my CCO would be sitting, I saw his things there, and took the chair next to him. He is a lovely man. He came and gave me a genuinely welcoming smile and sat there like it did not matter.

You have no idea how much courage it took to take that seat, stay there and behave like I owned it. Week in, week out. It got a bit easier. And after a while, like everything else, I had normalized the idea that this was my seat. This was my rightful place. And if I came in late, it was left vacant for me. But that first week and the weeks that followed, I knew for a fact that there were many who judged me for taking that seat. I could feel their eyes boring through my back and their whispers about who I thought I was, taking the choice seat next to the boss. What gave me the

---

[11] Carol Frohlinger and Kristi Hedges, 'Sheryl Sandberg On Why Women Need To 'Sit At The Table', *Forbes*, 2011, https://www.forbes.com/sites/work-in-progress/2011/01/18/sheryl-sandberg-on-why-women-need-to-sit-at-the-table/?sh=126b29d86de9.

right to take that seat? Honestly, nothing did. I took it because it was my right to take any seat I wanted. And I was not going to back down, no matter how much I felt like an imposter. That is the one thing you need to learn. What people think of you does not matter. And even how you feel inside sometimes is what has been programmed by others. Do not wait for others to *allow* you to take a seat. The spotted zebra carves the seat it wants to take and makes itself comfortable in it. At first, the seat is new, so it may feel a little strange. But once you get used to it and own it, others will start buying into your belief. They will respond to your confidence and accept your actions as normal.

Building Seats for Those Who Follow

But as the years went by, I realized it was not enough to take my seat at the table. Often, there are not enough seats at the table for women. Advertising is a boys' club. The men occupy most of the seats. There are not any left for women. So, I decided to build tables and chairs, and invite other women to take their seats.

Having a daughter made me care less about keeping my job or the stability of my environment and more about doing what was right by my conscience, for her future and for others around her. For two years of my life, I had to work under a male British boss who was in Asia for the first time. His idea of women in Asia was stuck in the Mad Men era, and he was sexually harassing women in my team with the universal excuse, 'I'm only joking.'

Each time I closed my eyes, I saw my daughter in the shoes of the person he was harassing. I started calling him out on it. I started saying out loud, 'That's not appropriate.' 'I am not comfortable with that statement.' 'That's sexual harassment.' I realized that it was not that he was audacious or incredibly bold. It was his power and title getting to his head. He came to Asia with a sense of entitlement. He told me once to my face, 'I thought Asian women are supposed to be subservient. What happened to you?' I remember turning around and telling him, 'You got off the time machine in the wrong era.' I complained to HR about him, and they went right back to him. I was not afraid. I knew word would eventually get to him. I wanted it to. I did not want him to think I was afraid of him. And it was not without its consequences. He made my life difficult. Work that was approved was thrown out, and I had to stay back and redo it over and over again. He had his favourites, and for obvious reasons I was not one, no matter how hard and smart I worked.

Defying the Popular to do What is Right

To be fair, I was not making it easy. I would have easily gotten promoted if I did not talk back and toed the line. But how could I not speak up? How could I in good conscience have a daughter and not stand up for myself and the women around me? I owed it to myself, my daughter, all the women in the room, and those who would come after us. I wish people had risen and fought these battles for me earlier. In just a few years, times changed, and policies were renewed after the '#MeToo movement', and the rise and fall of many advertising veterans. You know what the hardest thing was? Realizing that what empowered him was not him. It was his posse, the group of people who stood by him, supported him, laughed at his jokes, and stayed silent when blatant inappropriate remarks were made. They empowered him and further perpetuated and encouraged the idea that when something bad passes off as a joke, it is normal. It is acceptable.

Just because something is normalized, it does not make it right. When someone feels bullied, hurt, or is insulted for their race, culture, gender, age, or difference, it is not okay. We owe it to ourselves and our children to speak up, to step up even if it costs us, to de-normalize notions and behaviours that are creating toxic environments. I found a strange thing started to happen when I started speaking up and saying I was not okay with his toxic behaviour. While some people called me a 'prude' or stated behind my back that I was not cut out for advertising, others sat up and took notice. When I was in a room, people did not crack inappropriate jokes, and female creatives preferred to be in the room when I was there. In fact, many would ask me straight out, 'Uma, will you be attending this meeting?' And when I replied yes, I could see the look of relief on their faces.

Despite being made to redo work, being told outright to my face that I was going to be 'punished for being defiant', I could go home, kiss my kids goodnight and sleep with a clear conscience. That feeling of knowing if someone replayed the CCTV of my life to my kids one day and had them see I was a brave mom who chose to do the right thing no matter what it cost me, was worth it. Eventually, my boss left. Eventually, people in his team got investigated for sexual harassment. Eventually, policies in the ad world changed, and there was a proper code of conduct set in place to help women feel respected and protected in their work environment.

Someone asked me this after I delivered a keynote at a big tech agency, 'Uma, do you think we are overdoing it? Are women taking advantage of this? Do men genuinely want this change?'

To be able to stand up against the norm, the first thing you must do is recognize the norm—both the obvious and invisible. See what is right and wrong about the norm. See what it is that is different about you and your opinion of it. Understand why you feel that way, and then, speak up.

It took me awhile to answer the question. It was a loaded question, and I wanted every word I said to be honest and true, to myself at least. Do I think the new policies that have been put in place are overdoing it? Does it take the definition of what men are allowed or not allowed to do in the workplace to an extreme? No, I do not think so. I believe, for years, women have been afraid to speak up, fearing they would miss that promotion, lose that job they are good at. So, now I feel, with stricter policies, they can finally feel safe. They know they can complain and have somewhere to make complains if they feel mistreated. The people who receive these complaints have an obligation to investigate and act. Their jobs are on the line too.

And yes, men will be angry and afraid. It takes time to unlearn the toxic habit of making inappropriate jokes, staring at someone's breasts when you talk to them, and making sexual innuendos or racists jokes. No one becomes woke and aware overnight. But when you know you could lose your job doing this, you put in that extra effort to behave better. There is a strong and much needed incentive that literally forces you to unlearn that bad habit. It takes tough, clear, powerful, and uncomfortable steps to weed out toxic behaviour. We should not feel bad about pressuring someone to reconsider their bad habits and become better, no matter how angry, upset, or uncomfortable it makes them, to create a better working place. I have had many sexual innuendoes thrown at me. I had my fair share of indecent proposals. The famous head of the horn section of an orchestra asked me, 'Would you like to come up to my room for a bit?' I had a boss ask me to come up to his hotel room and show him my work. I told them both, 'No, thanks.' Well, to be precise, I told the first one, who was a whole lot older, 'Eew! No thanks, grandpa.' And I literally told the second one, 'Bugger off!'

The worst was when a short French man, who was working on a project with me, said to me, 'You know what would really sell this idea? Show the client your boobs.' I snapped. I turned around and looked him straight in the eye and asked, 'Would you like someone to say that to your daughter? Or is this the kind of advice you'd give her when she's older?' Everyone in that room told me to contain my temper. Surprisingly, no one asked him to gargle bleach and clean his filthy mouth.

I told my kids about the struggles in my agency. I was teaching them about sexual harassment, right and wrong behaviour in the workplace and how they should not behave in this way nor tolerate anyone who does. I also explained the importance of standing up and speaking up for people with no voices. I remember the day I was sharing my story. We were on holiday in New Zealand. My husband had just driven and parked in a lot in Queenstown city centre, when the kids jumped out of the car as we got out and hugged me tightly and told me, 'Mom, we are so proud of you. You are very brave.' Tears filled my eyes. Then, my son asked me, 'Mom, you're really good at what you do. Why not quit and go somewhere else? Why are you letting your boss bully you?'

I turned around and told my kids, 'Listen carefully. That's what most people would do. But mom is very good at what she does. And apart from my boss, I enjoy my work. I like my colleagues. So, I am not going to let someone intimidate me or drive me away from doing what I love in a place I love. If anyone should quit or be asked to leave, it should be him.'

This is another thing that society often tells you, 'If you're faced with hardship, throw in the towel and quit.' The spotted zebra knows its rights. It never quits doing what it loves because of someone else. It makes decisions based on its passion and what it believes to be true. A spotted zebra braves hardship to do what is right, even when everyone thinks it should take the easy way out and quit.

If you are faced with hardship, embrace it, learn from it, and stand up to your oppressors like Moses, the Prince of Egypt. Know your place. Know your purpose. Stand in the authority given to you. Do not let anyone take that away. No one has the power to reduce you to nothing, except you.

And here is the spotted zebra lesson from this chapter. When you want to see change, you need to do something different from what is popular or expected. Speak up against what is wrong and be willing to live with the consequences. You cannot change the world without paying the price. And even if you do not see immediate change around you, paying the price always changes you for the better.

Chapter 7

Turning ADHD into a Superpower

As you might have noticed, I have mentioned my clinical ADHD a number of times in the book already. I am unabashed about it; after all, it is an integral part of who I am. However, would you believe me when I say it was only in my mid 30s that I finally found the courage to tell people I have clinical ADHD? Seriously. I was afraid I would be looked down upon and everything I do would be looked at through the ADHD lens.

But until this book, only close friends, my husband, and I knew how I was diagnosed with ADHD. I do occasionally mention it in passing; people laugh, they think I'm joking. So, yes, if you are reading this book, consider yourself privileged. You know something about my life that not many people have known till now.

But when I finally spoke up about having ADHD, a lot of creative people started reaching out to me. I am a high performing ADHD sufferer. I have learned to use the power of visualization, positive thinking, staggered ideation, and multi-doodling to keep my focus and communicate clearly. Today, kids are allowed fidget spinners in class to keep their focus. I remember during university, when I was fiddling with my pen during lecture, despite being the most active listener in class, the one asking all the questions and challenging the notions, the professor walked over, grabbed my pen, chucked it aside, and asked me to pay attention. Well, this is how I pay attention. I shake my leg to a rhythm. I go into intense meditation and a place of peace, by headbanging to rock music. I flick my pen and swing it about to get into a cadence that allows me to concentrate. And sometimes I concentrate so deep, I forget where I am mid-sentence or while presenting an idea. I start getting up and running off towards accomplishing that idea. It is strange, comes across as rude sometimes, and surprises people around me. More often than not, I leave everything I brought behind.

On my wedding day, Brenda, the bestie I mentioned in the earlier chapter who was also my maid of honour, stood up and gave a speech and talked about how she used to pack my bag for me when we were in school. Honestly, I never knew that until that moment. And then when I heard it, I realized all these years, that was how my bags got packed. My husband, sitting on my right, laughed at what she said and joked how he is my new Brenda.

Today, they have tapping exercises and other forms of active actions to induce concentration. Back in the day, not sitting still at your desk, fidgeting, and moving or shaking in your seat were seen as disruptive actions. It did not matter that I was a high performing student who got good grades. I was still seen as an outcast. So, I would focus on keeping it in. The thing with focus is that when you give it to a single thing, everything else that matters suffers. So, I had to choose: am I going to focus on pleasing the people around me and adhering to their rules of sitting still and staring at the board like everyone else, or am I going to let that go at the risk of being labelled disruptive, and focus on learning? Guess which this spotted zebra chose?

It took some time and I learned to pick my battles. It also influenced the classes I took. I gravitated towards lecturers who allowed me to be me and welcomed my flurry of energy, questions, and excitement. And the ones who considered me unruly and frightening, I missed their lectures. It was a shame because some of those subjects really piqued my interest.

You do You, Foibles and All

Today, I think ADHD is a part of evolution. We have a generation that does not know what life is without mixed reality. They cannot imagine a world without the second screen. They were born multitasking to parents who are champion multi-taskers. And they have developed shorter attention spans. Some people see it as a problem. Research shows[12] memory is a system created by natural selection. It exists in its present form because it is able to solve certain recurrent problems faced by the humans in our evolutionary past. This means memory evolves and takes on a new form when we need it to meet the new needs of today. We have less of a need to memorize data today than we did in the past. That is because we have tools that help us store information and access them easily. We do not need to know how to do complex math. We just need to know which tool will assist us with the complex math. Now our synapses are being trained to re-evaluate what is priority. Priority is no longer knowing what to do. Priority is finding the right tools that will help us uncover the answer. I like that. It means we are not just storing information. We are storing ways to learn new things and keep on learning and discovering new tools. I do not remember all the names of the stores that sell great shoes in Asia. But I remember all the 'phrases' to key in to Google to find them.

Yes, we could all end up stupid if there is a tech meltdown and we cannot access our tools. But we would also all end up dead

---

[12] Stanley B. Klein, Theresa E. Robertson, and Andrew W. Delton, Summary and abstract of 'Facing the future: Memory as an evolved system for planning future acts', *Publication Manual of the National Library of Medicine*, (PubMed Central: 2013), https://www.ncbi.nlm.nih.gov/pmc/articles/PMC3553218/.

if there is a nuclear meltdown, yet no one spends time talking about that. But we all talk about the woes of technology to a generation that is evolving mentally and physically because of it. Good or bad, the purpose of this book is not to take sides on this argument. But I do believe we need to stop and acknowledge change. We need to acknowledge that technology and the access to fast information and how we digest information and entertainment has changed. We may or may not be okay with it. But we must also acknowledge that the same way we drive cars and not ride horses on roads, there is a generation that would prefer to access information via YouTube and Google instead of books. And you may not like it. But it is okay. The end objective is accessing information for whatever purpose we need. We must not let society dictate how we do this. We must find our own way of doing this, the way that is right for us.

My son taught me this when he was just eleven. I walked into his room and caught him on his iPad and started yelling, 'Daniel, you've spent the last hour on that device. When are you going to put it down and study for your science test?' He yelled back, 'Mom, what do you think I'm doing? My notes are on my iPad, and I have links to YouTube videos with lessons on the different topics. It's much easier to watch than read. I can learn faster.'

I was taken aback. And that familiar feeling of not wanting to lose to your own child crept up, and I replied, 'Well, reading your science book will make you smarter.' Yes, I do realize how dumb what I said to him must have sounded, as I type this sentence. I was spouting what generations of parents have said to their kids under similar circumstances without considering the meaning and value of what was said.

My son, however, was not inclined to textbook answers. Wonder who he got that from? Society tells us follow data and research, listen to the experts and their interpretation of it. I learned over the years from the school of life to read the data, hear the experts out, but follow your gut in making the ultimate decision. It is your choice and the only person you are allowed to blame is you. And I teach my kids the same thing, which makes them harder to handle, as I discovered in this situation. But I can only hope and have faith that because of this, they will grow up to be better people.

Daniel had a quick comeback to what I had said. 'Mom, I do not judge how you gather information. Let me gather mine my way. So long as I learn what I need to, what does it matter to you how I do it?' I could hear the silent Beyonce snap in my head. And my son tried to keep his cool, but I could see a smile escaping the corner of his lips when he realized he had gotten the better of me. I could hear my husband on the other side of the room guffawing.

Thanks to the constant barrage of digital exposure, ADHD is more common than you think. Both our kids have it to some degree. My kids, however, exercise no mercy when it comes to pointing out my ADHD moments. And when I do not do something that appeases them, they go, 'It's your ADHD, mom. It just makes you say and do these weird things.'

In fact, a lot of conditions are common today. In the past, pre-technology humans were one-dimensional. We understood our five senses to be our only senses, the only way we see the world. But we are not physical beings anymore. Technology has set us free. The simple act of putting on a Virtual Reality (VR) headset tricks our brains into thinking we are somewhere else, doing something dangerous or exciting. We feel real fear or experience heights in a real way whilst standing in the safety of our living rooms. It goes to show, we are more than our physical senses. We are multi-dimensional beings who also exist in a virtual world, and in some ways, our bodies are evolving to adapt to this world.

Personally, I can see both my kids have different degrees of obsessive-compulsive disorder (OCD), attention-deficit disorder (ADD) and ADHD. But it is what makes them awesome at navigating the virtual world, for digital and virtual natives, being born with this is *not* being born with a condition. It is their bodies evolving and developing to live in the new world they are born into. They need it to survive this environment, and yet, as parents, we fault them and try and take away the very thing that they need to excel in this new world. Instead of vilifying ADHD and similar conditions, it is time to openly admit it, help each other, and find ways to use it positively.

During the Covid-19 lockdown, the world saw an increase in mental illnesses. Organizations had to spend money to help their staff stay connected, feel needed, have a break from work. It had me wondering how many were already suffering pre-pandemic but never got a chance to ask for help. Why did it take a pandemic for companies to stop and not only think about the economic wellbeing of the organization but also take notice of the physical and mental well-being of their staff?

Create Safe Communities for Others Like You

As I started speaking openly about having ADHD, friends as well as complete strangers in the creative circle reached out to talk about their conditions, to ask for help, and get coping strategies. This was pre-Covid, and an Executive Creative Director friend had lunch with me as we discussed and exchanged notes on the condition. I asked him what he does on the bad days. He said he just calls in sick or sometimes loses his cool and has a breakdown. I asked him why he did not want to talk to his bosses. He was afraid of losing his job. In my mind, I was thinking, a white man in Asia, afraid to lose his job. God help us brown Asian girls with mental conditions. I wish I did not think that, but that is the reality of our circumstance, is it not?

But that is not the point. The point is, I was glad to have spoken up about my condition and have people reach out to me with theirs. Contrary to society and its beliefs, we should not hide our conditions. We need to own it—the good and the bad. It is what makes us who we are. I wish I had come out earlier and spoken about my condition. There were times when I recognized it in others but did not want to broach the topic, in case, I had to admit to having it myself. But I should have. It should be okay to talk about our differences, our issues, and our state of mind openly. Why is it taboo to ask for help? Why has it become a shame to show our vulnerability?

I have come to see my ADHD as a superpower I can tap into when I need it. Like now, in writing this book, between running a very busy ad agency, solving client crisis, leading the singing in church, sitting in the exco for the Global Leadership Summit Asia (I hate boards. I get bored being part of boards, so I am still figuring how I got into this one.), writing raps about Elon Musk (do not ask), helping my kids with school work—Grade 8 math and literature and Grade 6 science, and emceeing and delivering keynotes for global events. It feels incredibly stressful just typing all I have to do in one sentence. But what enables me to plough through, no matter how exhausted I am, is my ADHD. In fact, the ability to do all these things simultaneously and having my mind organize the information in a creative manner—it is all possible because of the way my mind functions, thanks to my ADHD. My husband has seen me on quiet days when I have nothing to do. Trust me, I am my best person when I am occupied in mind, body, and spirit. You know that saying, 'The idle mind is the devil's playground'? It is true. When I have an idle mind, I become the devil and drive everyone around me nuts.

Nothing is more effective than ADHD when you must come up with ideas at high speed. Let me describe what it is like to try and sleep with ADHD. You are lying in bed, or attempting to. You turn on your sleep app, and you start meditating on the music and hope you drift off into lala land. Instead, your mind starts figuring out the chord configuration of the music. You start calculating the beats per minute of its rhythm. And then you realize one of the 'Go to sleep' lines being narrated to you is grammatically incorrect. But you are not sure. You jump up. You go back to the exact point to rewind and listen again. By now, you are fully awake, and you realize you have got an idea for that project that is only due next week. But you do not want a good idea to slip away. So, you turn on your MacBook and start doing some research. Research turns into a full-blown deck. One idea becomes two, then three, and then the alarm rings and it is the next morning. That is my every night. But for some reason, when the alarm rings, all I want to do is sleep. Like my mind wants to do the opposite of what it is expected to do. But then when I try and sleep, there is this other part of my mind saying it is morning, you should be up. Stop lazing. And the cycle of madness, growing big hairy ideas, and lack of sleep continues.

It was far worse when I was a child. When someone asks me a question, there are thousands of mini bouncy balls all bouncing together inside my mind. The balls are hitting each other and knocking the other off as they try to escape a narrow door. So, while the wild ideas are constantly expanding and growing in my head, bursting to come out, they never quite make it out of the door. I struggled to present my ideas, to get my thinking out. Sometimes, I trip over the ideas. Sometimes I skip steps that are crucial to communicate the idea. Over the years, I have learned to focus my thoughts.

Reaping the Fruits of Your Flaws

My clients now laugh and say they can literally see the idea wheel spinning in my eyes when they speak to me about a brief, and my thinking process starts. Earlier, I used to just zone out when thinking and clients used to think they had lost me. It took time, patience, practice, and telling them I have ADHD to get to this place where I can have the space to process, think, focus, and present my thoughts in a way that clients understand. It means a lot when people are willing to give you the space to think and the opportunity to be brilliant without misunderstanding you and thinking you have completely zoned out. Now people who know me know that I have gone deeper into processing what they are saying. Instead of just listening to the brief, I am, in my mind, playing 'consumer' and walking through the journey and experiences as I am being briefed. I am entering rooms inside rooms—my mind is like the films of my favourite French director Michel Gondry.

I am grateful to have arrived at this place. And I feel this incredible need to grab people who are lost in their own conditions and thoughts like I once was and tell them that it is okay. It is not a problem. It is a superpower. Do not beat it down and hide it. Let it rise to the surface. Understand it and work it to bring out the best of you.

Of course, there was that one time, when I was presenting to a multinational client, when in the middle of the presentation— just as the client looked pleased and was about to buy into the concept, and the account servicing lead (we call them suits in ad land) looked excited at the notion of an idea sold so easily—I stopped presenting and looked at everyone in the room. The suit was giving me the death stare, asking me to continue. I flipped through my deck quickly, then looked at the clients and said, 'I can't do this. I'm sorry. This doesn't work. This idea is so boring, we owe you better.' The client was taken aback. The suit was angry. I was just bored. Incredibly bored. I had bored myself with my idea. I asked for a couple of extra days. The clients said they liked the idea but would like to see how I can make it better. The suit came back and complained to my chairman who called me to his room. I thought he would scold me. Instead, he just stared at me for a few seconds before laughing out loud. He said that right after we left, the client called and said he liked how candid and honest I was. The client told him that for once in his life, he felt the agency was not just there to sell him stuff, but to give him an idea we believed in. He looked at me and said, 'Your crazy worked. And now they love you. So, go do your thing. I will manage the suit.'

I was not sure if I should have taken it as a compliment. I had to burn the midnight oil with my mildly annoyed and incredibly amused team because of the stunt I pulled. But the result was a better campaign and a client who suddenly started trusting me a whole lot more. It also became a running joke each time I paused to gather my thoughts at presentations—everyone was sure I was going to tell them how much my own idea sucked and ask for an extension to present a better one. It was a funny situation born out of my condition, but I did not apologize for it. I just went with the flow. Sometimes, that is the best we can do and it is okay. Well, in this case, it was more than okay—the lead client and my chairman developed a newfound respect for me overnight. The suit, on the other hand, walked into every meeting with me in trepidation, no matter how much I tried convincing her that there was nothing to worry about.

The spotted zebra teaches you in this chapter that you need not look at your condition as an impediment or an imperfection. Look at it as evolution to cope with the life you are living and the circumstances and technologies you are exposed to.

The psychologist I met told me my ADHD is probably my body's way of coping with whatever I am experiencing to help me retain my sanity and emotional stability. It was my survival mechanism. When I look back, I think he was right. Without it, I would not have survived. Which means, you would not be reading this book. Your body knows how to evolve to help you thrive in the world you are living in. It is not for someone else to tell you if you are okay. They are not walking in your shoes. You are. So, make the most of who you are and all that you have.

Chapter 8

Bring Diversity not Because I Look Different but because I Think Different

We are in an era where gender fluidity as well as racial and gender diversity are being pushed for and recognized as human rights policies. Companies are feeling the pressure to hire for diversity. Just a few years back, I was fighting to be heard for my own sake and my children's. And while the situation is not fixed, now is really the best time to be a brown, Asian, female entrepreneur and executive creative director. I have given many keynotes on the topic in Sweden, Australia, Pakistan, Nepal, Mongolia, and, of course, Southeast Asia at various global and regional summits. It is trending.

Bandwagons, Innovations, and Being Your Unique Self

But one thing I have found is while we are keen to bring a variety of colours and genders to the table, we are not always open to a difference in thinking and ideation. Apple's tagline has always been 'Think Different'. They have not changed it since the late, great Steve Jobs launched the Apple brand ad, 'Here's to the crazy ones'.

He named his company Apple—after a fruit. Now this is cutting edge, unique, and unexpected. He went against the norm.

I call Steve Jobs the godfather of my kids. Why? Well, up until recently, my family has been diehard Apple fans. We use the Apple home system and willingly pay for all Apple products because of the quality and the service we get, and we support the brand because it leads in my ultimate criteria of what any good product should have—design that is simple, clean, seamless, and cool, this includes the typography—and user experience. I want more than efficiency when buying a product. I am not buying user reviews. I am buying a feeling. How it makes me feel when I use it. And more than that, how it makes me feel when I am seen carrying it around and tell people I own the said product. It is more than status. It is that sense of belonging to a community—a group of people who are different from the rest—and are like me.

This is something a lot of marketers do not get instinctively. We need to stop being marketers. We need to be users first to sell our products. At KVUR, the advertising agency I co-founded, when we think of ideas for clients, it always starts with the problem we want to solve and what the solution feels like.

We remember things, moments, experiences, and interactions by how they make us feel, as users.

Psychologists work with dementia patients to help them remember themselves and key moments in their lives by creating triggers like smell, pictures, and songs that make them feel emotions that would trigger memories[13]. Deeper than logic and information is the power of the emotion. It lasts.

The late Harvard Business School professor Clayton Christenson authored *The Innovator's Dilemma*. He later went on to author *The Innovator's Solution*. These are books that every marketer

---

[13] Federica Savazzi et al, '"Art, Colors, and Emotions" Treatment (ACE-t): A Pilot Study on the Efficacy of an Art-Based Intervention for People With Alzheimer's Disease', *Frontiers*, 2020, https://www.frontiersin.org/articles/10.3389/fpsyg.2020.01467/full.

should read. Do not take my word for it—take Steve Jobs'[14]. He often referred to it for his Apple product development and marketing strategy.

It is a very dry book and written in a very academic manner. But once you can get past the style of writing, there are plenty of pearls of wisdom in there. One of Christenson's key insights[15] is that people are not loyal to brands. They are loyal to themselves. And they buy products and services from the right brand that can meet their needs best at any given time. So do not sell your efficacies and your product superiority. Sell a solution to answer people's requirements and dreams. And if you can get their attention by showing them what that solution feels like, they will come to your store and give you their money. A classic example of this is NFTs. People are buying NFTs to clothe their avatars, to style their gaming characters, to decorate their metaverse space. Yes, it is investment as well. But why are we chasing something that is not physical? Because what people deem as real does not have to be physical. It just has to provide the right feeling. There is so much value in emotions. Society for the longest time told us to think soundly, to make rational decisions. Yet the strongest driver for anyone to take action, is emotions. We were born emotional.

But how do you find out what the emotional drivers are? Christensen in his book talked about understanding the job that needs to be done. Basically, what are the motivators of these people? And while it starts off looking like it is purely functional, when you drill deeper, you find the emotional motivation and need, and that is the job to be done. In simple words, the job to

[14] James Allworth, 'Steve Jobs Solved the Innovator's Dilemma', *Harvard Business Review*, 2011, https://hbr.org/2011/10/steve-jobs-solved-the-innovato.

[15] 'What Job Would Consumers Want to Hire a Product To Do?' interview of Clayton Christensen by Dina Gerdeman, *Harvard Business School*, 2016, https://hbswk.hbs.edu/item/clay-christensen-the-theory-of-jobs-to-be-done.

be done is the most basic problem you need to solve, the single base need which your product or service can meet. Beyond that, you need to show that your product or service is *the* best choice in meeting that need, otherwise why would they spend their money on you and not someone else?

So, how do we find this out? Christensen conducts 'jobs-to-be-done interviews'[16] to get to the 'why' of their behaviour. And the objective or output is not listening to what people are saying. It is listening deeper to what they are not saying. Instead of asking questions, you get consumers to describe their user journey. After hearing a few consumers describe their journey, if you listen deep enough, you see a pattern form—a pattern that reveals their 'why' and their 'where'—all the touchpoints that helped them make their decisions and the types of questions at each touchpoint that instructed, enforced, and triggered their decision. It is qualitative research on human behaviour and decision-making. I have conducted many of these interviews as part of my Master's programme research for design thinking in Innovation and Technology.

One thing I learned from research was the power of observation, which is another key thing that helped me identify the job to be done. It was not just what they said, it was how they said it and how they looked when they said it. I could tell which was true and which was being said because the interviewee thought this was what I wanted to hear.

If you are a marketer reading this book, this little nugget was thrown in just for you to show the power of arriving at the right data to help you sell. So, how is this different from a focus group—because in a focus group the data you collect is based

16 'What Job Would Consumers Want to Hire a Product To Do?' interview of Clayton Christensen by Dina Gerdeman, *Harvard Business School*, 2016, https://hbswk.hbs.edu/item/clay-christensen-the-theory-of-jobs-to-be-done.

on what people tell you, not from what they are not telling you. And for humans, the truth may not be absolutely true, we tend to colour it with the filters of our experiences and expectations. We can't help but tell our version of the truth because of social conditioning.

I have attended hundreds of focus groups over the years. And at every focus group I find there are these three groups of people:

1. The Freeloaders

They have nothing better to do. You are paying them a couple of hundred bucks. They are getting a free meal—it is a break from having to cook for the family after work. The husband is agreeable because wifey is bringing back extra moolah from sitting down and having a chat about her ideas with a bunch of other ladies. And if the husband is out, the wife is happy, she gets to Netflix and chill while hubby is out of her hair for a few hours. So, they are there to enjoy the meal, collect the money, be agreeable, and say something nice about whatever you show them.

2. The Anarchists

I love these. They are highly argumentative and unbelievably entertaining except when they are tearing apart the campaign you have spent many late nights on, simply because they can. They are angry at the world and have told themselves no matter how much money you give them, they cannot be bought. Now, do not mistake these people for spotted zebras. They are not being different or unique. They are just being difficult. And they are open about it. And they are not doing it subtly either.

So, they will take the money, gobble down every last morsel of their free meal, and then say the opposite of what everyone else is saying. They are always the minority because God-forbid they seem agreeable. They do not want theirs to be the popular opinion. But their voices are the loudest, their protests the clearest, and their 'No, I do not agree with you' unmistakeable. Even when they secretly agree with the majority, they have made up their minds that today, at this hour, in this room, they are going to exercise their right to be and do the opposite of everyone else.

I know these people well because that is how I was as a teenager when my parents asked me to do chores. I had to do it. I know there was no escaping. And honestly, deep down I knew it was my responsibility, but I did not like doing it. So, I made it my life's mission for that hour or more to let my parents know exactly how I felt, much to their annoyance. My teenager and tween do the same to me now—talk about karma and reaping what you sow. I really need to find a way to break this cycle. It might be my next book. But for now, back to focus groups and its next category of people.

3. The Sheep

Their motto: Why think when you can follow? They have had a long, hard day. They are amicable, easy going, and hate to rock the boat. They are the last to speak. You are not sure whose side they are on at first because they are agreeing with counterarguments that are complete opposites. But with these, you need to wait till the end because they do pick a side—the side of the majority, the winning side. That is the plan. Go to a focus group. Hear everyone out. See where the popular opinion is leaning towards and sway in that direction.

So, everyone comes to a focus group with a pre-conceived notion and plan on what they are going to do and why they are there. I have had close to 250 previews—a preview is when you test an advertising campaign for almost every market at a focus group, to find a winning concept. I have also personally attended at least thirty previews, and I have found this to be true every single time.

Guy Kawasaki's story of the Sony boombox focus group[17] is yet another proof of why they do not work. When Sony wanted to sell their boombox years back, they invited a bunch of people for a focus group, to ask them what colour boomboxes Sony should make. They had to pick between black and yellow, and they all said yellow. Sony made bright yellow boomboxes and they never left the shelves. So, after a few months and not seeing the results that they wanted, despite having an awesome product, they brought back the same group of participants. They asked them the same question and got the same answer. This time, they asked the participants to head down to the factory and pick a free boombox. And guess what? Everyone picked black. Sony went out with black editions and the boomboxes sold like hot cakes.

What went wrong? People talk a lot at focus groups. But no one tells the truth. I am not saying people are blatantly lying. But I think at focus groups, personal agendas outweigh true opinions.

So, why trust a focus group to determine the success of your brand campaigns? And for those reading this who are not marketers, keep this in mind when you are making life decisions based on data that is printed. People like you and I inform focus groups with our hidden motivations, some of which we ourselves are not aware of. Perhaps, it is time you tried something different, like instead of making decisions based on what data says the majority are doing, go with your gut instinct. Sony only got it right when they stopped asking and started observing. You know what is best for you. So, what if it is different from the majority are saying? Follow your heart. At least if it is the wrong decision, you know that wrong decision is yours. Own it. Laugh about it. Tell stories to your family and friends about it.

---

[17] Joe Natoli, '4 Reasons Focus Groups Don't Work', *Give Good UX*, https://givegoodux.com/4-reasons-focus-groups-dont-work/.

Diversity, Feelings, and a Sense of Belonging

In his talk on *Synthetic Happiness*[18], Harvard professor Dan Gilbert speaks of how choices are one of the main causes of unhappiness. The more choices we have, the more we cannot decide if we made the best one. My husband is a classic example of how this is true. He comes home after buying something and then keeps thinking about the five other variants he could have chosen but did not. It seriously occupies his thoughts. And then he goes back to the store and changes it a few times. And then always goes back to his original decision. Going through the process of buying, changing a few times, and going back to the original is his process of making decisions. Yes, it is painful and tedious. But it is therapeutic and reassuring for him. One thing is certain, if I owned a shop, my husband will not be allowed to shop in it.

I am grateful for my ADHD. I have no patience for options. I will pick the first thing I see that meets my criteria. It may not be the best decision, but it is a decision that I can live with, born out of me thinking different from everyone else. Uma thinking like Uma. But the average human, when given options, behaves more like my husband. You have to only pick the one. You walk away unsure if the choice you made is the right one. And even when you have read that this is the most popular one and you follow that data, you still could come home with it and feel unhappy about your choice.

That is because humans are not just data driven; we are passion driven. I would have picked a black boombox too. Not because black is my favourite colour, but because if I am going to walk around with a boombox, it needs to match my swag outfits. I have lots of colours, I need my boombox to be an accessory that does not clash. So, black would be the easiest to match. It is probably the

---

[18] Dan Gilbert, 'Synthetic Happiness', YouTube video, posted by Trà Dương, 8 Nov 2007, https://youtu.be/eLKfTgG_9Ok.

same with the others—when asked what colour they would pick, they thought on behalf of others and thought that the brighter colour would sell. But when it became something they could own, the decision-making criteria changed. Now they probably had to think if it will look good in their home. Everyone has their own coloured walls and décor, so black is the easiest to match. Now this is all based on my assumption. None of it is based on facts, but you might look at my hypothesis and agree, which brings me to my next point—when you need to gather data from a focus group, you assume the set of questions you ask will help you arrive at your answer. But you only have an hour or two, and you can only ask so many questions. It is impossible to find sufficient questions that could get a diverse group of individuals to arrive at the singular goal you hope to achieve via the answers they provide.

And here is the other thing. Even if we arrive at the right data, human beings are not data driven. Are you data driven? Do you make all your decisions based on information you are provided?

I certainly do not. If I did, I would be the slimmest, fittest person on the planet. Yet despite my weighing scale telling me 'one at a time please' and research saying women in their 40s should cut back on carb and sugar, the giant scoops of Belgian chocolate ice cream that occupy my freezer still find their way into my mouth. We are famous for quitting one vice by taking on a new one. Have you met the smoker who quit smoking by eating salad? No? I have not either, but I have met the smoker who quit smoking by drinking more alcohol.

This is also why diets do not work for long. Humans swap one bad habit for another because we are junkies for emotional highs. To sell a product, as an advertising creative, I try and create an emotional high. To succeed in life, you cannot just blindly follow the data out there. You know it is not going to work. You need to find the emotion that drives you and find something positive that feeds that emotion.

I decided to lose 10 kgs post Covid because there were so many nice clothes I wanted to get into. And yes, my blood pressure was incredibly high. I knew I had to lose weight to get it down. But I knew that high blood pressure was not reason enough to lose weight. I needed more. So, I found clothes I love and started buying them. After spending the money on the clothes, I had no choice but to lose weight so I could fit into them. Problem now is, I have lost more weight than planned and some of the clothes are a bit loose. I need to take them to the seamstress and have them adjusted. But that is the truth. You need to find an emotional motivation to meet your goals. And it cannot be something generic. The emotional goal must be something unique to you.

Data is not wrong. It is important to have data. But it is how we interpret data that will make the difference. The problem is marketers are selling products and services based on efficiency, product efficacy, and superiority. Governments and schools have made this the end objective. Beyond making me *think* why this is right for me, make me *feel* why this is right for me. That is why Apple's 'Think Different' ad worked. It broke so many conventions and spread an unconventional notion that the computer—used to do all these important, analytical things—was not just the property of stuffy people in suits.

The Apple ad did more than sell a computer brand. It sold a feeling of inclusivity, acceptance, and broke barriers. It made skin heads, people with tattoos, the rebels and misfits of society feel that they were intelligent and did important work and were worth acknowledging. It was a nod to the folks who were sticking out. It elevated them to a place where their difference was seen as what made them stand out from the crowd. It was an ode to the spotted zebra—at least, back then, it was.

Apple today, in my opinion, has fallen into the wormhole of peddling minute product enhancements versus ideas, emotions, and innovation—these things which epitomized the spirit of the forbidden fruit was long buried with Steve Jobs.

Now there is a very important lesson here. The purpose of diversity is not to fill a quota or be seen as a forward-thinking organization to up your PR value. The objective is to have people who think different at the table. It is to increase the number of unique ideas. When there is a diversity of ideas, you have sufficient ingredients on the table to come up with a great output. When there are the same types of ideas—no doubt they may be good— after a while, they get stale and bland.

I saw this happen in advertising. In the early days of advertising, or of everything, actually, the decision-makers were men—white men who looked, behaved, and thought a certain. Now I do not hate white people. My granddad was one, so technically I am one quarter white. I am just stating a fact which we are all familiar with. This was the same for advertising. But advertising has set the stage and paved the path for a lot of things—how men and women should behave at home, at work, and in social environments; what clothes to wear to look cool; what cool looks like. What is beautiful? What is right and morally acceptable? What behaviours should be shunned? What constitutes a faux pas? Advertising set the stage on the parameters of what a successful human being looked like—a white man living standard, which the world quickly adopted, from the West to the East. We did not know better, and times were different. I am not going to judge history. We evolved. Well, not fast enough, but we did.

But the thing that stuck out to me was how, in advertising, in the early days, the judges of all the award shows were men. The parameters that define what creativity is and what a good idea looks like is seen through a male lens. I am not saying there is anything wrong with a male lens. But when it becomes the only lens, we have a serious problem. This resulted in only a certain type of idea, humour, and creativity being accepted as good—the gold standard. The parameters and rules for creativity in general became very male. You had to think, create, and execute a certain way to be deemed creative, to have your idea pronounced as good—and that certain way, was a male way.

And in my early days of advertising, I thought this was the only way. This was the right way. Because it was normalized and programmed into me. I used to think about ideas from a male perspective. Even when I was doing ads for Wonderbra, washing detergents, and shampoo, I looked at it from a male lens—what my male bosses would see as a good idea, the kind of idea that would get a nod from the male jury and help me pick up an award.

This is exactly why a lot of men get hired for creative roles in advertising. Because when young female creatives who have yet to be 'programmed' to think this way present their books at job interviews, the creative director puts a male lens when he judges her portfolio. He is thinking this does not look familiar. It does not fit the mould of what the judges are looking for. If I hire her, she will not get our humour and creativity. She is not going to help me win an award. And this type of thinking is exactly why there are not as many women creatives in advertising, but you do see many in account service.

It is not because women aren't creative. It is because we create differently from men. Now, I never saw this until I had a son and a daughter. I started seeing how, from the time they were born, they were both incredibly creative. But the way they ideate, create, and come up with concepts and art is so different. I used to come home with my creative briefs and challenge them to solve it for me. They loved the exercise. Little four- and six-year-olds running off with paper and colour pencils. Then they will come back with 'BIG IDEAS' to show me, trying to outdo each other. And I was always so surprised how different the concepts were. But as we grow up and start becoming institutionalized, we start force-fitting our thinking into a very narrow mould and decide this is what creativity looks like. This is what 'award winning' looks like. But when we formulate creativity and force fit it into a mould, can we still say it is creative?

Showing How Different Is not Wrong

When I was at Ogilvy, I got tired of being told my ideas were too sensitive and 'only a woman would think like that', 'why are all your ideas for women and saving women and elevating them?' For the sake of my children, I started the Female Idea Movement to spread the message that ideas are not gender neutral. They are male and female. They are both awesome and equally important. In order to have the best ideas, you need a pool of both ideas in equal—or near equal—numbers. And in order to have a pool of equally good ideas that are male and female, you need a diversity of creatives at the table to give you diversity of creativity and creative thinking. Campaign Brief[19] reported the recent number of female creative directors to sit around 17 per cent. A lot has happened in the advertising world with #metoo and the dethroning of many male advertising greats for sexual and financial misconducts, tyranny, or the simple act of pleasuring oneself on a zoom call for all to see whilst thinking the video was off. There has been a conscious drive by big agencies, especially those in America, to increase the female quota, Zippia reported[20] that this year, the number of female creative directors in the US are up to 41.8 per cent. I am curious to know what that number is in Singapore and the rest of Asia.

---

[19] Candace Kuss and Ali Hanan, Creative Equals: Future Leaders 2021, *Campaign*, 2021, https://www.campaignlive.co.uk/article/creative-equals-future-leaders-2021/1715551.

[20] 'Marketing and Creative Director Demographics and Statistics in the US', *Zippia*, *https://*www.zippia.com/marketing-and-creative-director-jobs/demographics/.

Thinking New to Disrupt the Norm

Think Different—it is a great tagline. It should be the mantra for companies when they bring people together to brainstorm—the single rule that should be the foundation of all ideas you come up with. Instead, from the time they are children, our kids are forced to toe the line in their thinking. The reason for diversity in race and gender is to have multiple ideas from different backgrounds brought to the table.

When I was growing up, my exposure to thinking was from countries that included Malaysia, Singapore, New Zealand, Hong Kong, Australia, the UK and America. My ideas of language and construct and communication was very Western. I thought if you spoke good English and communicated clearly using good grammar, you are a good communicator and that is how you succeed.

The one thing I loved about advertising and working in a multinational organization was, despite having old white boys call the shot, in an agency like Ogilvy where Singapore was the APAC hub, you saw a lot of diversity. People may not have the best command of English, but they have great insights to impart. I learned that English is not a superior language. It is a tool for communication. And you do not need a strong command of a language to communicate. You need clarity of thought and the ability to construct and structure your message in a way that wins the hearts and imagination of people. And I have found some amazing ideas born out of people who can barely speak English. This also made me proud of all the languages I speak outside of English—Hebrew, Bahasa Malaysia, Bahasa Indonesia, and smatters of Cantonese, Teochew, and Tamil. And when I travel, instead of being embarrassed if I am speaking incorrectly, I try and pick up as much of the local language as I can and strike up conversations. It is not about getting the accent right; it is about communicating your intent and building a connection.

This is why schools have it wrong. The focus on languages should transcend just grammar, vocabulary, and perfect pronunciation. It should be expression and communication. There is so much power in this, and more students would be interested in learning a language for the love of learning and communicating. The exams should not be on paper—you should send kids out with tasks to a shop that only speaks Chinese and see if they can use their linguistic skills to complete the task. Is not that the purpose? Not everyone becomes a language scholar. Right now, just for love, and out of curiosity, I am learning Spanish and Vulcan—a language spoken by an alien race in Star Trek—on Duolingo. A spotted zebra knows that the drive to learn something new is not grades, it is love and curiosity.

We need to be open to different thinking and different ideas. When we understand why they are needed, we will not care so much that our ideas are different from everyone else's or that other people's ideas are different from ours.

The Apple brand that Jobs concocted was an extension of him. If you watched the docudrama *The Pirates of Silicon Valley*[21] about the founding of Apple and Microsoft, you would have watched the scene where Jobs, after many failed attempts to get a business loan, agreed to cut his hair, put on a suit, and see, if this time, by conforming, he could get a loan. He did. They signed and gave him the money—nothing to do with his capabilities or business plan. The look of success was put in a tiny box for these bankers. It was the criteria of whether they would approve a loan or not. Once he got the loan, he proceeded to build a brand

---

[21] https://en.wikipedia.org/wiki/Pirates_of_Silicon_Valley

for the misfits—all the people who do not look the part to get loans approved by banks. He created a cultural revolution in the business world and revamped what success looked like.

I remember, for years, I held out from buying a new Nokia phone, even though my mobile phone was falling apart, because the iPhone was going to be launched. I wanted to buy the new iPhone because it was cool. Jobs was not selling product-efficiency or convenience. The iPhone has all of that. It was a smart mobile device—not just a phone. But I held out and waited for it because it made me feel like I could step into something new and better because of it. I did not know the details of the iPhone. Yes, Steve Jobs was there giving the Apple keynotes and talking about the functions. But I was not listening to any of it. I was feeling his passion, excited by this promise of us entering a new era of connected devices (although honestly, I had no clue what that meant fully, but it felt right), and I wanted in on it. This was even better than the promise of 10,000 songs in my pocket—yes, I had that, and it was awesome. Now this was so much more.

So, the day after I gave birth to Daniel, the iPhone was launched in Singapore. I did not mind being in the hospital alone. It was auspicious that my son would be born in this era where a mobile phone was not just for calls and texts. I made my husband leave me and queue up for an iPhone. That was my baby gift. Daniel played with my iPhone quite a bit. He named it Bob after the 'Bob the Builder' app on it. When Obama came on TV with his campaign rally cry, 'Can we fix it, yes we can', the kids actually thought he was Bob the Builder.

And when Sarah was born, the iPad was launched. In fact, her first word was iPad. It sounded a lot like dad—so I was a tad jealous. But peace was restored to my home when she pointed to the iPad on the TV console and said 'iPad', 'iPad'. And that is why I had mentioned earlier that Steve Jobs was their godfather. Steve did not know it. But the kids did. I always talked to them about the spirit of innovation and the notion of thinking different that their 'godfather' had shared with the world.

Redefining Beauty to be More Inclusive

Recently, I caught the drama series *Colin in Black and White*[22] on Netflix about the life of American activist and former NFL quarterback Colin Kaepernick. In it, Kaepernick narrates his life story and takes us through his formative years, navigating race, class, and culture while aspiring for greatness. In Episode 5 of the series, he talks about how, for years, beauty was defined as blonde, blue eyes, and fair skin, and he was made to feel uncomfortable about dating the incredibly dark-skinned girl he had a crush on even by his black friends.

When popular culture defines what beauty, greatness and success look like, society walks around wearing the lenses of that definition. They enforce those lenses on us. And we start thinking we need to fit into that definition. We force the people around us to fit that definition because we want them to succeed in the world we live in and that simply means conforming to what people want. But when we do that, we lose the value of who we are, our uniqueness. The spotted zebra loses its spots—the thing that makes it a spotted zebra. Sometimes this is simply because of the people we see around us. What looks normal to us becomes the standard by which we feel obligated to live our lives.

My kids went to an Australian pre-school in my neighbourhood in Siglap in the east coast of Singapore. My daughter who has a beautiful golden tan came home from school one day and said, 'Mom, why can't I be peach?' It broke my heart that she should want to be anything other than who she is. I asked her, 'Why do you want to be peach? You have golden

---

[22] *Colin in Black and White*, created by Ava DuVernay and Colin Kaepernick, (Netflix, 2021), https://www.netflix.com/sg/title/80244479.

skin like an Amazonian warrior. You are special and beautiful. No one else looks like you.' And she said, 'But all the other kids have blue eyes, blonde hair, and peach skin. I just want to be like them.' It took a while, but I started talking to her about how being different is her special power. I also talked to her about aliens—and how they would look different from us if they showed up and that does not mean they are not beautiful. We talked about all the different coloured skins and people. We even talked about how animals look different and beautiful because they are colourful. So, I was very happy when she started buying dolls of different colours with funky hair and cool shoes. I was not so happy when she started painting her expensive dolls blue and purple. Now she has outgrown her doll phase. Thank God for that. I always thought they were slightly creepy. Now Sarah is into baking complex deserts, which is especially bad for our domestic helper's waistline. She has also proudly and wholly embraced her golden-brown skin tone. A big part of it is what is being normalized by the shows on streaming services. Kudos to companies that push to show diversity in gender and skin tone. Sarah watched the recent Miss Marvel series where a brown, Asian, average sized teenage superhero is seen coming into her powers and dealing with her complex teenage relationships with peers and family in a healthy way and I can see the positive impact the series has on her.

I worked on a campaign called Afrostats at Ogilvy, where we used different afro hairstyles as charts to talk about how people of African descent in Western countries are being ostracized because of their natural hair. It was an education for me. I did not know that in some organizations you cannot wear your afro au naturel. It is deemed as unprofessional. So, you have to straighten it, tame it, or crop it ultra-short to be allowed into the office. And in Hollywood, a lot of African American hosts had to pay to straighten their hair to stay in their jobs. Many stars have spoken

up on how even when they style it, it is deemed 'too black'[23]. I was
just appalled by how the powers that be would deem the very thing
you are born with as unprofessional or inappropriate. I was even
more appalled that this was legal. How is saying black people's
hair is unacceptable any different from saying black people's skin
tone is not acceptable? It really goes to show that people judge
you for being different and not just because of your gifts, talents,
or behaviour. They pick on you for who you are and how you
are made. The only cure for this is to own your difference and
be proud of it, irrespective of what people say, and normalize
the idea that it is okay to be different. In fact, it is beyond okay;
it is good. It is great. It is what makes this world that much more
colourful and better. You make the world better by owning you.

One of the most powerful things I recently heard was a
podcast[24] by Jay Shetty, former monk, author, and purpose coach.
Jay said very aptly that we develop our opinion of ourselves based
on people's opinions of us. We think we are what they think we
are. If they think we are stupid, we think we are stupid, and we
start behaving in a way that makes what they think of us become
a fact. If they think we are violent, we believe that and think and
manifest it into our reality. The biggest problem with society
is that we outsource our opinions of ourselves to others. And
therefore, we outsource our self-image to others. People do not
know us. They judge us based on a five-minute interaction with
us. Or our race. Or our friends and family. Or the one project they
worked with us on, when we were slightly off our game. That is
not the totality of who we are. You and I have a responsibility to
allow our uniqueness to shine to show the world who we are. We

---

[23] Paulina Jayne Isaac written, Khaliha Hawkins reported, '18 Famous Women on
How Hollywood Still Can't Get Black Hair Right', *Glamour*, 2021, https://www.
glamour.com/gallery/celebrity-hair-discrimination-stories.

[24] 'Dwayne Wade & Jay Shetty on Letting Go of Validation', *Jay Shetty*, 2022, https://
jayshetty.me/blog/dwayne-wade-and-jay-shetty-on-letting-go-of-validation/.

cannot let someone else define who we are. Stop outsourcing your self-image to someone else.

For generations, we—governments, parents, and educators—have also been responsible for introducing and normalizing this notion that you do not own your self-image, someone else does. When do we do it? When we tell our kids 'Stop doing that, *people* will think you are rude' or 'Do not talk so loudly, *everyone* in this restaurant will think you are uncultured.' When we do this, we are building into our children the notion that the objective of good behaviour, doing the right thing, following instructions is merely to please, satisfy, and get the nod of approval from those around us. We are outsourcing our children's self-image to the people around them and giving them the wrong idea that this is how the world works. I am guilty of this too. That is why I was careful to write 'we'. Instead, what I am trying to do is help my children take responsibility for who they become. The objective of good behaviour is not to get the approval of society. It is nice when people say good things about you. I will be the first to admit it. We all crave admiration and attention, especially as a parent, seeing your child being praised for something good is great. But that should be the by-product, not the focus. Now when they misbehave, I tell my kids, 'Is this how you want to behave? Does this bring you joy? Your actions are mean, and they are hurting me. I know you are not a mean person. Being kind is a choice. Why not choose differently next time?' Teach them to own their self-image, that every decision they make is to better themselves and become the best version of them. Not what others expect them to be.

This brings me back to the need for a diversity of ideas. It does not just fall on parents and educators. Governments and corporations need to consciously take steps to ensure there is diversity of thinking. Make diversity a part of the hiring quota wherever possible. A global mindset means becoming open to people from diverse cultures working with you. Start with gender equality and cultural richness. Make the boardroom table a place where ideas from all walks of life and all parts of the globe meet—a cross cultural melting pot of great thinking. Be open to the notion that some things are new and unfamiliar. Allow for and welcome the new and the strange. Just because you do not know it and it is not the way you have been doing things in your workplace does not make it wrong. No one starts off knowing what *better* looks like. You only know something is better after you have tried a new idea, given it enough time to take effect, experienced the effects of it, and can deem whether it is positive or not. Then you can gauge if it surpassed the results of what you were previously doing. Sometimes you might have an inkling of whether something is going to work.

Stepping Back to Make Room for Possibilities

There are many times when I have worked with my creative teams and pronounced an idea as awesome only to execute it and realise it is not working. But this is okay. There are lessons to be learned even from bad ideas. And there were times when I felt something was a bad idea and was tempted to pull the plug on it at inception. But then I saw the eagerness of the young creative presenting it to me, or even my kids insisting we need to try it. I tell myself, 'Oh well, I am going to root for this to work, but I am not sure if it will'. And despite my doubts and what my previous experiences showed me, it worked amazingly well.

In 2010, Elon Musk and SpaceX became the first to launch a privately built space capsule into orbit and return it safely to Earth[25]. Believing space to be the next frontier for mankind, Musk announced that he wanted to be the first entrepreneur to put an

---

[25] Steven Siceloff, SpaceX Launches Success with Falcon 9/Dragon Flight, *NASA*, 2010, https://www.nasa.gov/offices/c3po/home/spacexfeature.html.

astronaut in orbit. Musk was a big fan of iconic Apollo astronaut Neil Armstrong, the first man to set foot on the moon. But Armstrong opposed and criticized him. He even testified before Congress to protest against the commercialization of space, saying it threatened American dominance in space exploration[26].

I watched the interview Elon Musk did in response to Neil Armstrong's testimony, holding back his tears, saying how he was very hurt and disappointed by what had happened. Musk, despite the outright rejection, got a new breed of experts— people who have never landed on the moon but are great engineers and physicists of future tech—to help send a team to the International Space Station. It was a remarkable achievement that the world celebrated. I watched the whole thing, swallowing every morsel of information, every piece of video released on Twitter and YouTube, and more recently, the documentary series called 'Return to Space' on Netflix[27].

Now, this is a key lesson from the spotted zebra. Most of us look to experts and those who have historically been figures of authority in sectors to help guide our decisions. But the reality is that with changing times, technology, and even consumer and environments, we cannot look to past knowledge, historic expertise, and approvals of heroes of old to guide us towards a new frontier and future success. History informs but it is not a guide. History is a reminder, not a trail blazer. We need fresh ideas, revolutionary thinking, and facets of thoughts that are different in order to achieve new, unexpected successes. It also means we need to be open to testing new ideas and innovation.

How do you create an environment where you can innovate?

---

[26] "Private Space Pioneer Elon Musk Counters Neil Armstrong, Critics on '60 Minutes'", *Space.com*, 2012, https://www.space.com/14936-spacex-ceo-elon-musk-60-minutes-interview.html

[27] *Return to Space*, directed by Jimmy Chin and Elizabeth Chai Vasarhelyi (Netflix, 2022), https://www.netflix.com/sg/title/81111324.

Take for example, Sarah, my twelve-year-old. She is an amazing baker. Not the kind where mom swoops in, assists and lets her do the final touch-up, and then posts pictures and pretends she has done an amazing job. She is the kind I can leave at home, come back from work, and see two trays of multi-flavoured cupcakes professionally iced, a tray of croissants, and homemade garlic Brioche—all made from scratch. As I had mentioned previously, she wants to study at Le Cordon Bleu, has catered for book launches, and sold her pastries and desserts for pocket money and to raise funds for her favourite charity, Team Seas. She has even contributed to her grandmother's knee treatment with her funds. But it did not start because she was born an amazing baker. While she definitely has talent and passion, I like to believe that I helped stoke that passion and created an environment where she could safely fail and learn. I understood what it meant to support her.

Initially, I bought the ingredients as she gave me the list of things she wanted to make. This was costly, especially when the output failed. But so long as she did not quit, learned from her mistakes, and tried again, I supported her. She got better, and now, she is able to pay for her own ingredients from the money she makes selling what she bakes. The spotted zebra knows that if you hang on to what you long for and allow for failure, you make room for new successes.

It is the same for my fourteen-year-old son. My husband and I decided to invest in his passion for design, creativity, and engineering. We got him a 3D printer which he could practice with. He was specific about what he needed. We bought him the software he needed to design and print 3D objects. He started making and selling things. He even 3D prints and sells mechanical gaming keyboards. He has made some amazing jewellery for me that I wear with my designer clothes and get massive compliments for. There were lots of mistakes, frustrations, and wastage in the learning process. But we wanted to encourage his entrepreneurial spirit and feed his desire to innovate.

Do not get me wrong. Both kids were informed of the consequences of their failures. I make it a point whether they want to listen or not, to tell them that when we threw away that batch of ingredients or resin, it cost us x amount of money. I tell them that it is the price of the lesson they learned. And then I ask them what lesson did they learn for the money mom and dad lost? What can they do better next time? It gets them thinking.

Sometimes, they are not sure what the lesson is. So, we create hypothetical scenarios about what could happen if it worked and other ways things could go wrong. Just sitting and hypothesizing is a way of learning. And then I tell them, if they can try again based on their learnings or hypothesis, I am happy to support them. Initially their greatest fear was, 'Is mom expecting us not to fail this time?' They did not want to disappoint me. I told them that it was fine if it did not work so long as they worked to figure out why and what they could do right, or simply better the next time. After a few tries, I noticed my kids went from 'I do not want to disappoint mom or waste her money' to 'Let me see if I can nail it the first time.' And as they got better at understanding the principles behind what they were doing, they got better and started becoming more adventurous in taking on more complex tasks—exactly what I wanted them to do. I want them to push the envelope, not be complacent about what they have mastered, and keep learning. And as a boss, I want a staff with the same attitude, constantly pushing themselves to try something new, pushing the boundaries of creativity, and pushing me to open my eyes and ears to their ideas, no matter how foreign and new they seem.

The spotted zebra knows innovation cannot happen without failure. If you want to do what is tested and tried, you will not innovate. If you are not willing to invest in people's ideas if it is not a guaranteed success, you cannot innovate.

When SpaceX first invested in reusable rockets, the first few exploded[28]. That was a very costly failure. But the fourth one succeeded and that one success was a huge leap in space travel innovation for mankind. Without those failure and learnings, we would not have the advancements made in rocket technology and engineering today.

So, if you want your company to have people who dare to innovate and think different, you need to allow a safe environment for them to fail. Success should not be the criteria for promotion and career advancement. If you want success from your staff all the time, they will take the tried and tested route. I ask my creative team to think of new, unexpected, untried things, learn new things, bring new technology and ideas to the table. That is what gets them promoted. Show me something I do not know, and let us try it and see if we can make it work. That is how you can do great things.

The main spotted zebra lesson for this chapter is that the more different ideas you have on the table, the higher the chances of progress, the greater the opportunities to grow, and the wider the net you cast. Because it is not about doing better what everyone else is doing. If that was the case, Nokia would have stayed in the game as the No.1 mobile device in the world. They kept engineering better phones. They felt they were on top and did not feel the need to do anything new. Just do the old better was their mantra. Keep what is working well. Keep doing it well. But maintenance is never the key to survival. The iPhone crushed Nokia phones overnight.

A culture of playing it safe without room for innovation, or rather room for failure, will end with your brand or whatever it

---

[28] Marcia Smith, 'Four Tries, Four Failures, But SpaceX Undeterred on Starship Tests', *SpacePolicyOnline.com*, https://spacepolicyonline.com/news/four-tries-four-failures-but-spacex-undeterred-on-starship-tests/.

is you are doing becoming obsolete. The faster you fail at many small things in its early stages, the faster you will learn fundamental lessons that will help you build the big things that will launch and propel you to greatness. I remember when my son first told me, 'Mom, I do not want to fail,' part of me wanted to hug him and say, 'You won't.' But I did not. Instead, I paused, thought my answer through and went with my convictions instead of my maternal instincts. So, you can imagine his surprise when I responded, 'Why not? It's the fastest way to learn.' And the more open you are to implementing different ideas you do not fully understand, the more chances you have of becoming a unicorn, a supernova, creating and becoming known for doing the impossible.

Chapter 9

Breaking the System if it is
Breaking the People

We are almost at the end of the book. I had started the book with my life journey, the things that make me different, and how I worked in institutions where I started discovering the strength of my uniqueness and the courage to use that uniqueness to make my environment better. As I moved up the ladder of influence, I found that I had taken myself to a place where people trusted me to shape cultures and restructure teams that are allowed to— actually, encouraged to—use their uniqueness and individuality in a corporate setting to produce amazing results.

When I joined Weber Shandwick to build a creative team from ground zero, it was scary, but it was also awesome. I could do two things—take my nineteen years of advertising experience and do exactly what I know or take those years of experience, break it down, and see what I can do better.

Taking the Bull by the Horn

On my last days at Ogilvy, Chief People Officer, Sue Olivier, said some kind words to me and gave me a book called *The First 90 Days* by Michael D. Watkins. It was a great book on how to strategize and succeed in a new role. And I digested it and decided

I was going to go through the steps and set the tone of what I wanted to achieve.

It started with me writing down how an advertising agency is run, based on my observations. Having worked at a small boutique ad agency called Crush and then at bigger agencies—McCann, Publicis, J. Walter Thomson (now just Walter Thomson), Euro RSCG (now Havas), Saatchi, and Ogilvy—I think this was the easiest exercise for me. There were things unique to each agency but there were fundamental constructs that the big boys had established and religiously observed.

Then I wrote down what I liked about the agencies. This invoked a lot of strong feelings and brought back key moments. I realized that while I could not remember the details of some of the moments that flashed back, I remembered the feelings those moments evoked, and they are as real today as they were when I was experiencing the moments. In fact, more real at times, because I can focus on the feeling of the moment versus going through it.

The strange thing was that it was not just the good, easy, fun, or happy moments that brought joy to my heart. It was remembering some of the arguments, the challenges, the late nights thinking I was not going to be able to crack an idea, working with people I did not like or could not stand that brought me joy. Why? Because of the reward of the outcome. These were arguments that helped me discover a new way to do something. I learned. The reward of walking into a board room with a great idea born out of collaboration and an overnight struggle was worth it. And finding out that the people I feared, shunned, and wanted to flee from had more in common with me and ended up becoming my friends after the long journey. Nothing beats the joy of having your enemies become your friends. And here is where the spotted zebra behaves differently. While the norm is to find the easiest way to do something, doing the hard thing is far more satisfying and rewarding. I am not asking you to look for hard things consciously and go after them. No, do not punish yourself. When you embark on a journey you cannot avoid and things get hard, do not quit. The steeper the learning curve, the harder the path, the braver you need to be, the stronger you become, and the more you grow.

One of my fondest moments was a pitch presentation practice session for a big brand. There were ten people in the boardroom. I was the creative lead for the pitch. I stood up to present the idea. The presentation was good, but this was my first tech B2B pitch, and I was using consumer jargons to explain my idea. I could see the look of horror on the faces of the people— all experts in B2B. My chairman stood up right after, in front of everyone in the room, 'If we lose this pitch, it's because of you.' My ears were burning. I was embarrassed, and everyone in that room literally looked at me with pity. I do not do pity. So, I smiled, looked him in the eye, and said, 'Okay. But if we win this pitch, it is also because of me.' He smiled back. I could feel the silent sigh of relief in the room. I did not go to a corner, cry, and throw in the towel. Instead, once everyone left, I turned to the head of planning and told him, 'You are not going anywhere. You are staying and helping me win this.' To his credit, he did. He helped me carve out my entire presentation with the right lingo, the correct B2B jargons. I worked hard that night to memorize every word and pepper it with my own creative essence and humour— because it was about servers and IoT, which can get dry. You need to hold the crowd's attention. The entire presentation went well, the head of planning watching me whilst beaming with genuine pride. I literally had to avoid his eyes throughout the presentation because I would have burst out laughing at his expression. We won the pitch. And my chairman gave me due credit, as promised. It was a very uncomfortable experience. But it was also a very sweet, victorious moment in my advertising career.

The next thing I did was write down all the things I did not like about agency life. Things that held me back from becoming the best me. Things I did not want to repeat. Then I stopped midway. Most people weigh the pros and the cons before they start something new. For me it, I realized as I was weighing the cons, if I just focused on the thing I want to do, inculcating a culture I believe in, I will not have time to do the things I do not want to do. My dad told me when I was young, 'Do not worry about doing the wrong thing. If you focus on doing the right thing, you won't have time for anything else, including the wrong thing.' Life is like that. Starting something new is like that. My spotted zebra moment was to focus on what I wanted to achieve, the culture I wanted to build, and the feeling I wanted to instil and grow. When I focused on these things, I did not have time to consider all the things I did not want to do.

Changing the System to Better the Culture

And so, I started my fledgling creative team in a PR company. I stopped thinking how a big advertising agency would run their creative teams. Instead, I started thinking, what would make the best creative team? How do I find hybrids, not just the traditional copywriter and art director? Why should I limit people to one role? Let them grow and try different things. And if, along the way, they should feel they are more suited for something different and they do it well, they would be more of an asset doing that than the original thing they were hired to do. I learned to be flexible and use people for their strengths. Everyone could share their ideas. Everyone had to contribute. It was not a walk in the park. When you try doing new things, you fail. But that is okay. You pick yourself up and pivot. I was so proud of every member of my team. People think it is about efficiency, structure, and planning. Yes, I had a lot of experience with creative teams, and I would like to think I was a good leader. But one of the key reasons why the team did well was because I chose to bury the sacred cows.

Things that ad agencies held dear and decided were crucial to what made a good creative team, but were not working or just unnecessary in this new setup, I chucked deliberately out.

The first was the copywriter, art director, and creative team construct. I mentioned this above. I looked for hybrids. Copywriters who could do basic video edits and their own voiceovers. Art directors who were great photographers, understood the ins and outs of gaming and blockchain technology. I did not want a creative team that could produce a big idea. I wanted a creative team that could create ideas for the new world, whatever is next, maybe even create that next new thing. But I was a realist in that. When someone came to me with a crazy idea, I would ask them to research the technology to make that happen, give me a realistic timeline—this can be hypothetical, a breakdown of steps to do this, and who they would need to collaborate with to get this done. I did not want to put an idea in front of the client that was overbudgeted and could not be executed. Ad agencies are notorious for this.

I had an awesome creative technologist who was used to building websites before I showed up. As soon as I knew his capabilities, I pushed him to do the impossible, including inventing paper thin rechargeable wireless mobile charges and smart bus shelters and outdoor devices that gathered data from Google and shielded people from the weather. We created some amazing experiences as a creative team.

My spotted zebra moment here: I did not have to be the smartest person in the room. In the world of big boy advertising, and any corporation for that matter, you cannot outshine the boss. You pay the price for showing that you are smarter than them. With my creative team, the smartest person in the room was not me. There were people far smarter, far better. And that is why we thrived. My gift was to identify these people and provide them with the platform to do the best work possible. When you have a boss that can do that—allow the smart ones to showcase their talents without feeling threatened and work together with others to produce great ideas—you have a winning team.

The second spotted zebra moment was when I chose to run my creative team like I did my family. This meant not throwing away the baby with the bath water. Instead, I enabled the baby to make it better. When I was in advertising, I was repeatedly told not to have lunch with my team, to maintain the hierarchy. But what can I say, I grew up on a farm, hung out with animals, had conversations with myself. There was no hierarchy. I was a socialist at heart who believed in the capitalism of ideas and intelligence. They knew I loved them, was proud of them, genuinely cared for them and had their backs. And if they failed and made a mistake, I would sit with them and walk through the learnings. I pushed them hard to be better. They got scolded when they came in late and were chided and pushed when I felt they were not trying enough. But I also sat and talked through their stress with them. I tried to help out with their personal goals and dreams, while building their own brand. Organizations talk about staff retention. Honestly, in this day and age, no organization can provide loyalty and benefits that our grandfather's company did. So, to expect that same level of loyalty our grandfathers gave their companies, without the remuneration being as desirable, is ridiculous.

And so, instead, I did the next best thing which I would have liked companies to do for me. I helped my team build their own brand. When they knew they would benefit from staying with me, at a personal level and at a level where their passion, dream, and ambition were being built beyond the company goals, they stayed. And they stayed loyal. Not because of the contract they signed. But because of the genuine interest and time I put in to help them become the best them. But it works two ways. You need to find people who are hungry to learn, grow, and want to do better.

Unfortunately, not everyone is this way. And I did meet some people I genuinely struggled to lead. Most young people may not be loyal to an organization, but they will be loyal to a good boss. So, we have an obligation to help them be the best version of themselves. It does not matter if they leave you in a year of two because you helped them get better. What matters is that during the year or two, you both grew and made magic together.

I learned a very painful lesson during my early years in advertising. I found a way to make something better. I formed this idea around a leaner, meaner creative process that was more efficient. I created a structure with processes and people in place. A methodology to crowdsource content and social-jack trending news and use it as ads for brands. It was new and exciting, and no one has done it. I was in an MNC, and I spoke to my boss about it. I was so excited and thought I had chanced upon a revolutionary insight. I tested the hypothesis on a few friends in advertising and they all thought it was fabulous and in many ways novel and fail-safe.

Then my boss announced my findings to the whole company. I was excited and I was waiting to be called on to lead the change, to implement the process, and, of course, get promoted in the process. You know, go from creative director to chief change maker or chief unicorn or something equally exciting. Weeks became months and nothing happened. I was frustrated. I had waited all this while, patiently, and now it was time to approach him. I did, reluctantly, afraid that I was going to hear something I would not like to hear. I was surprised by how candid he was. He told me to take this as a learning moment. That while my idea was good and could be implemented, and I was probably the right person to implement it, he did not want to change a system that was working. People were used to the old way. It was something everyone was familiar with. Introducing something new is risky. It means training people to behave in a whole new way that they were not accustomed to. And nothing was harder than changing behaviour. System changes, technology changes— these, even though they cost money, were easier to implement.

Changes that required a shift in human behaviour could result in unhappiness, unwillingness to learn, and a mass exodus. I asked him, 'Wouldn't it make things better?' He said, 'Yes, undeniably better. But I am satisfied with how things are going. And a lot of people want to carry on doing what they are doing because they are succeeding according to the standards set by the company. They might fail if they did it a new way and that would jeopardize their next promotion.' I realized at that point that he was referring to himself and his career growth too.

Most people do not want change. Not if you are a worker in the company. Not if you are hitting all the basic requirements of the system. You are accustomed to it. You have mastered gaming the system. Why would you want the system to change? Even if it makes things better for the company and is good for business and profits, if it is not good for your immediate career progress, and you will resist it.

That was my spotted zebra moment. I realized that I cannot initiate a system that is different and better, alone. As a leader, I need to inculcate the notion that everyone has to think of ways to improve the system and link their career progress and key performance indicators to this. That way, they will be incentivized to change. They will see change as benefitting them directly.

Recently, I started taking my son and daughter to see a physiotherapist and a chiropractor. I did this because I noticed my son's posture was getting worse after his runs. Daniel is a cross country athlete. He had been complaining a lot about body aches, especially on his calves and ankles. When I took him to the chiropractor, the first thing he said was that my son suffered from very stiff hamstrings. The stretching exercises the trainers were making him do during practice were not enough. He had to stretch deeper and longer to loosen his hamstrings. We had a physiotherapist work with him to achieve this. The first few days he suffered from great pain. He was not used to the deep stretching. But I had to push him to keep at it. Most parents would have quit by now and taken the easy way out, blamed the physiotherapist saying they were making their child worse.

Instead, I researched the situation. I know as an exercise junky myself how much it hurts when you first start doing new moves. You just have to bear with the pain, keep at it, build your muscles, and have your body get into gear, slowly but surely, to support your moves. I also chanced upon the story of Tiger Woods, the famed, shamed, then re-honoured golf legend, who decided at the height of his career to get a better trainer and change his swing[29]. With his new swing, it took him some time to regain his game. His body hurt. He was not winning as many championships because suddenly his swing had changed. The game had shifted. But after a few months and putting in the hard work, he returned stronger than ever, regaining his title. He could have stayed the same and plateaued. His only motivation to change his swing and get a better trainer was his desire to learn, to be better, to become the best golfer there was.

I told my son this story, to help him understand why he was going to the chiropractor to get fixed, how this was going to make him better. The chiro told him plainly when they first met, 'Once you manage to loosen up your hamstrings, you will be able to run more effortlessly.' I hung on to that promise. And a month later, my son told me that he too felt it was easier.

Breaking Rules that are not Worth Keeping

No one wants to fix something that is not broken. But the spotted zebra recognizes that there is a difference between making something work and creating something excellent. And despite the inconvenience, the pain, the temporary fall from glory, to make something greater, you have to break the mould.

---

[29] Matthew Rudy, 'Tiger Woods' swing evolution', *Golf Digest*, 2021, https://www.golfdigest.com/story/tiger-woods-swing-evolution.

Yes, all the striped zebras will bitch about you. They will call you a fool. But once the tide turns, and the profits start rolling in, they will say you're a maverick. And the same who insulted you will claim that they believed in you from the start. What gave me the courage to break rules was hanging on to the principle that rules were made for people, not people for rules. Unfortunately, when these rules become irrelevant and no longer apply, they start doing harm. The system that was set up to protect the people or improve their lives is now destroying them. The predecessors who made the rules have died. And the successor is too afraid to change it despite the damage being done.

This is often the situation in governments, education systems, and organizations. Governments need to be progressive. Unfortunately, most great governments like great countries start off with a founding father, a visionary who drove change. But when the successors take over, they fall into a maintenance mentality. They dare not bring about change. They want to keep the rules of their forefathers. But what worked before may no longer be relevant. And if you do not break the system or evolve it with time, you are breaking the country and its people. Change will come to governments and businesses. Change is a force of circumstances, of socioeconomic climate, and how that effects the lives of people. If governments do not change and adapt, they will no longer be in power.

As I write this, I am reminded of a Bible verse from Matthew 9: 14–17, 'You cannot put new wine in old wineskin.' From a political and corporate perspective, this simply means you cannot run a new world using old parameters, constructs, containments, and laws. Times have changed, the people, like the new wine, have changed. They are fresh, they have new ideas, new needs, new ways of living and being. The old rules, aka the old wineskin, do not apply anymore. And if the wineskin is not renewed, it will burst.

So, what is the lesson for the spotted zebra here? A simple one. Be brave to write your own rules on your own terms. Do not be perturbed by what people think of those rules. Hold your course. It will pay off.

Chapter 10

Owning My Difference—My Glory, My Shame, and My Fuckups

We are a religious family. Well, not from a traditional perspective. I grew up observing Judaism and a very Jewish culture. I observed a kosher diet. I believed Christ was the Messiah. And I do my best to live according to Biblical principles. I know, you are probably thinking, didn't you get physically and emotionally wounded by Christians and the Church? Yes, I did. But I also had two of the most Christ-like people I know pick me up and help me regain my footing with love and commitment. They are my parents. Benny and Naomi. Two of the most amazing human beings I have had the honour of encountering.

In previous chapters, I mentioned how I embraced my difference, picked myself up after a very dark chapter, and made something of myself. I did not build my life on my own courage, self-confidence and capabilities. I honestly feel I owe a big part of who I am and what I became to my parents and the God they introduced me to through the lives they lived. Their belief system and unconditional love empowered me in so many ways to become who I am today. And I would like to share a bit of that in this chapter.

As I mentioned in the earlier chapter, my dad has passed away. My mom is currently in Malaysia. My kids adore their grandmother. And no one is as devoted as her in praying for our family. When I have a crisis, she is the first one I call. As a mom and wife, I spend so many hours managing my home, taking care of the kids, being the responsible one. But just the knowledge that I have a mother who cares for me, reminds me I am not just a mom, I am a daughter too. And that as much as I pour all my love upon my kids, I too deserve to be loved.

The God I Know

While my idea of God was introduced to me by my parents and the religious institutions I was part of, over the years, I have grown my own view of God, based on my understanding of the Bible and life experiences. After my encounter with my godfather and a cult of people dictating who and what God is, I have started reading the Bible for myself. Because if you, like me, believe that one day we will be accountable for all our actions, you want those actions to be your own, based on choices you made; not based on what somebody else asked you to do or societal pressures. And I have decided to take God out of religion altogether and put Him in all of life.

Here is my idea of God. I warn you, it is a little out there. But I am not embarrassed about it, and I do not apologize for it for it is something I strongly believe in. The more I understand innovation, science, physics, and technology, the more I feel God, and my understanding of who He is, makes perfect sense. To me, He is an alien, a multidimensional being who created the universe we live in. Anyone who is not from this planet is technically an alien after all, right? Therefore, if you believe in an 'out-of-this-world', 'all-things-are-possible' kind of God, then my idea of Him cannot be discredited either.

Prayer to me is voice activated command. Like when you say, 'Alexa, turn on the aircon.' You know Alexa is going to do it.

You have faith in the technology that powers Alexa. So, when you come to God in faith and pray, you believe it is going to be done. And if it does not happen, you know there are real, solvable, and possible reasons why. As you might have guessed by now, I no longer subscribe to the belief that 'God works in mysterious ways'. I will likely never believe in it again. It is nothing more than a convenient excuse and mindless promise by people who are too lazy to make an effort to fully understand a situation. I emphasize that this is just the way I see things. I still strongly believe in the power of prayer. And as a parent, it is my therapy and my daily go to, to deal with parenting and life.

I can however grasp the notion that there are things God is doing and reasons for Him doing it that are beyond my understanding, for now. It is like science—there are lots of things that we hypothesize. We do this in theoretical physics all the time—we hypothesize aspects of creation that we have not been able to prove or fully understand. God, to me, is like that. There are so many things about Him that we can only hypothesize. And that is okay. Einstein said some preposterous things back in the day which are only being proven true today because of how technologies have advanced, and we can study things that we could not in the past.

Finding the Creator in Physics

Having spent a lot of time listening to and attending lectures and talks on String Theory by Professor Michio Kaku (give me a documentary on the black hole anytime over a romcom), I find that the idea of a timeless God, a God who was and is, and is to come, is explained by science more so than theology. Admittedly, it personally baffles me that theologians study scripture to validate their understanding of God but fail to study creation to understand God the Creator. Scientists however do this very well.

And without intending to, Kaku's lectures often help me make sense of and be in awe of the creator God of the Bible.

I also think of visions and apparitions as mixed reality. We spiritualize everything. But who is to say that all the visions described in the Bible are not a manifestation of mixed reality and this creator God does not have advanced technology at his disposal, seeing as how He is all wise and all knowing?

What does religion have to do with anything, you ask? Well, it has to do with everything. We all need to have a fundamental belief system. What we believe in dictates the principles that govern our lives. I am not dictating that we should all believe in the same thing. You are responsible for the choices you make. But that is exactly why you need a belief system. *You* are responsible for the *choices* you make. What do you think guides these choices?

Yes, a belief system. You must have a belief system that you own. In Singapore, I see people adopting the belief system of their forefathers because it is easy. We claim not to stand up for what we believe in because we are pressured to behave a certain way. To study a particular course. To take a particular job. We do it in the name of 'Honouring our elders', 'Respecting our culture', and 'Being responsible'. I spoke to a young woman a few years back who got defensive and said, 'You do not understand what I have to go through. I must study this and take this job I am not keen on because I need to support my family.' I felt sorry for her, because she had shackled herself to someone else's expectations, or so I thought initially.

But over the years, I have spoken to many young people who interviewed with me for creative jobs and even had meals with adults who have confessed to doing the obligatory thing for years. I also mentored and gave talks to many young graduates who are making that decision on what to do next with their lives. And I realized this notion of 'I have no choice', 'My so and so wants me to do it', or 'I have to do it for the sake of my family' is mostly an excuse. We do it because when something goes wrong, we have someone else to blame. This is a real shame because that is far from the truth. You may be blaming someone else when things go wrong in your life—your mom, dad, husband, wife, or a close friend. But do you really think that when you are sitting in despair, curled up with tears running down your eyes, or at the verge of bankruptcy, the person you are blaming is going to own up and accept the blame or swoop in and rescue you from your debt? Deep down you know the only person to be blamed for your choices and actions is you. And the only person who has to take responsibility and lift yourself out of the cesspit of hopelessness is you! And this is exactly why you need a belief system that is your own. It will serve as the North Star for your actions.

The Need for a North Star

My North Star is my Bible. Not my church's interpretation of the Bible. Not a theologian's interpretation of the Bible. Not what a bunch of Christian books on Amazon say about what God says about my life. Now do not get me wrong. I do read those books. They do present to me different facets of what the interpretation of the Bible could be. But I make my own decisions. I decide how and which parts inform my belief system and my idea of who my God is and what He wants me to be and do. Ultimately, my belief system is formed by what I read and understand the Bible to be.

I own my truth, and it guides my decisions. Every night when I lie in bed, I check myself against my belief system and go to bed with a light heart knowing I have acted according to it. I do not go to bed feeling great every night. Let us face it. We are not perfect and we make mistakes. Sometimes, I get the feeling I could have done something better. In such cases, I either make it right immediately or the next day, or if I cannot, I ask God for forgiveness, I forgive myself, and decide I will do better next time. My belief system does not make me perfect. It guides me to make better decisions and live a better life. I like that I have guiding principles I can check my life and actions against. That feeling that I did something wrong—it is not a bad thing. It is good. It is a reminder that I am human. I am alive. I have a conscience. It keeps me humble, reminds me I am fallible and capable of doing stupid things. And trust me, there is nothing more human than doing stupid things.

A spotted zebra does not let anyone else tell it what to believe in and how to act. You own your belief system and live by it. It makes you better. It makes you make the world around you better. You do not just exist. You show up and take responsibility for every moment you go through. And by just doing that, you change for the better. And you change the world around you.

Evolving in Your Belief

The thing about owning your belief system is being willing to admit when you are wrong. When I came out of the situation with my godfather, I was adamant to move away from everything I had learned that had hurt me in a deep way. I wanted to know God and understand who I was for myself. Along the way, I built some strong fundamentals that I held on to very tightly and then I did the very thing I hated people doing to me. I started judging people based on my belief system and enforcing what I believed on others in a rather draconian way. I decided who would and would not be my friends and what was morally right and wrong based on what I believed. Along the way, I came to learn that everyone has the right to live their truth. And it was not my place to judge them. Their lives and their actions would be the judge of them. I was only called to live by my truth and love those around me. That was a big lesson for me. The spotted zebra does not judge other zebras for their stripes as much as it does not want to be judged for its spots. And the spotted zebra is willing to change its beliefs when it realizes what it believes in is misguided, vain, or simply wrong. It is not an easy thing to do, but it is the right thing to do.

It is the same for laws of countries. They are the belief systems of a government. We should not hold on to archaic laws simply because they are the laws we have adhered to for years. The death sentence is something many countries have abolished, but some still adhere to it. What benefit do you get from taking another life? How does it support democracy and demonstrate a progressive nation? Nothing shows progress like grace and compassion, mercy and kindness. More than anything else, this is what society needs today. Is it not the job of a government to help enable better societies and civilization? How can laws of countries be revamped to champion grace and kindness?

Keeping Your Spots Requires Work

We all need our own belief systems. This is our anchor, our North Star. In the Old Testament, the patriarchs and the matriarchs created memorial stones at different points of their life. It was to honour a journey they had made and write down the lessons they had learned along the way. At different milestones of our lives, new memorial stones are set up and new lessons are learned. It is a constant journey of discovery, evolution, and growth. As a spotted zebra, you need to look back at each key moment of your life and remember the memorial stones you have set up. At each memorial stone, write the lesson you have learned, how it applies to you, and how you can apply it to make life better for your family, your colleagues, and your society.

You need to have your own unique lesson that defines who you are, which nobody else can own but you. When you own your belief systems, and are able to live by them, you will not be pressured by society to conform at key moments of your life. You have a strong foundation to stand on. You are free to be your true self and make decisions and take actions which you know to be right for you.

And the most important lesson for the spotted zebra here is that this journey of uncovering new lessons and setting up new memorial stones does not end. It continues all your life. And as you make that journey, you will discover more new uniqueness that make you a spotted zebra.

Chapter End

Reflections of a Spotted Zebra

Since I started on the journey of writing this book, it made me reflect on my life and learn new lessons. I started thinking about what it means to be a spotted zebra in our endemic climate. I had to read many books and watch many films and documentaries by people I recognized to be spotted zebras, as part of my research.

I read Maye Musk's *A Woman Makes a Plan*, Peter Thiel's *Zero to One*, and watched Colin Kaepernick's *Colin in Black and White* docudrama on Netflix. Maye Musk is an amazing author, businesswoman, and model in her seventies and the amazing mom to three highly successful children—Kimbal, Elon, and Tosca. Peter Thiel is one of the co-founders of PayPal, a German-American billionaire entrepreneur, venture capitalist, and political activist.

I had mentioned Kaepernick in an earlier chapter. This American civil rights activist and former football quarterback kneeled during the national anthem before games to protest racial injustice and police brutality against African Americans. *Colin in Black and White* is easily one of the most inspiring series I have watched about racism and the subconscious mistreatment of people of colour and the result of ignorance and lack of representation of the human race in totality. I watched it with my kids, and I need to give it a shout out. They are not big documentary watchers, but they were so engrossed in the series, I literally had to pull the remote off their hands and turn off the TV to get them to bed. And I can understand why. My children are two brown kids with Chinese surnames and a combination of too many races, living in a country that is primarily Chinese, where you do not see enough representation of kids that look like them. I have never seen two kids prouder of a country. They think Singapore is the best place on the planet. When we travel, they are the best ambassadors this country can have. Since they were little, I watched them describe with pride the great country of Singapore, where they are from. But I also know that looking and being different does bug them. Meritocracy is not enough to help people feel they belong. Community is. And this is only made possible by representation.

Coming back to the spotted zebras I mentioned above, each of them had a similar way of telling their stories. They unveiled key moments of their lives and peppered it with lessons learned and the message they wanted to get across. It was very easy and almost conversational, which was what I wanted for this book and attempted to do in the chapters you have read.

But while I came with the attitude of telling my story and sharing my lessons, my sharing exercise became more of a learning exercise. In writing this book, I discovered so much about myself, and realized that many of the things that I believed in had changed— yes, I discovered new belief systems that were stronger and better, and I uncovered areas I need to work harder on or be better at. And so, I thought I would share my reflections and my new discoveries during my writing process in this final chapter. I have divided it into eleven points to make it easily digestible. Why not ten, as people usually do? Hey, I am a spotted zebra. Random is good.

1. My difference is a mirror. The more I talk about it, the more I amplify it.

When I started writing this book, I spoke to tons of people. Many asked what the book was about, and I told them stories from the book and started discussing key spotted zebra moments. What surprised me was that even the most naturally conformist person I spoke to said how important this book is, especially for their children or the next generation. And then they started talking about their own spotted zebra moments. When the spotted zebra comes out and shows itself, other spotted zebras will see themselves in it and be drawn out.

2. My difference is something I should be proud of.

Being different is something to be proud of. We are not cookies out of a cutter. We were made unique and different from each other. I think of humanity as different pieces of a puzzle. When we come together, we create the full picture. But if a piece of puzzle behaved and looked like the other, we will never have a beautiful, complete picture.

When you are different, sometimes you are ashamed to show it. You try hard to be like everyone else, to blend in. You see this in every Hollywood superhero movie. In X-Men, Cyclops was ashamed of his powers. His parents considered him dangerous and a freak. They feared him and wanted to call the mutant task force to take him away, before he escaped and was rescued by Professor X who taught him how to own his powers, control them, and channel them for good.

It is the same with our uniqueness. We want to fit in. But when we are proud of our difference, we can stand out instead of stick out. Owning, talking about, and using my uniqueness makes me feel empowered. But if I was really honest, for a long time, I hid everything about me. My allergies. My ADHD. My opinions regarding God, religion, politics, and the environment. I tried to be 'normal'. I tried to be politically correct. Socially acceptable. But when you are a spotted zebra, it is hard to hide the spots. You suffer and feel oppressed. And people around you will spot the difference (pun fully intended).

It never feels easy to show your spots. I never feel comfortable saying I have ADHD or voicing my ideas that go against popular opinions. But the more I do it, the easier it gets. And when I do it with confidence, people start accepting it without a fight.

I remember once when I was invited to a costume party. The theme was Star Wars. I did not read the text from my friend properly. I saw Star. I saw space. And I showed up in my Star Trek crew outfit. The red and black one that Captain Picard wore on the USS Enterprise. Now, there is an ongoing rivalry between the fans of these franchises. Trekkies and Star Wars fans do not like each other. Star Wars is about storyline, cinematography, and capitalism. Trekkies love the geek-speak, the physics, science, and the socialism. So yes, I literally beamed myself into enemy territory that day with a sign across my chest 'Set phaser to kill and shoot me.' It was crazy. But I decided to be proud of the Trekkie I am. I am not going to apologize for dressing like my favourite captain of the Enterprise. I was going to own my 'shame' and turn it into 'glory'. And by that simple shift in attitude and perspective, I had so much fun that night. And so did every Wookie, imperial army and resistance recruit, Vader, Yoda, and droid in that place. I would be lying if I said they accepted me with arms wide open. They mocked me and tried shaming me. But I gave as good as I got, and we laughed, drank, and discussed the superiority of Star Wars vis-à-vis Star Trek the whole night, and they insisted I come back to every Star Wars party they organize in future as a Star Trek captain, just so the night would be that much more entertaining.

3. My difference is not just for me. We need to embrace our difference—for ourselves, our family, society, and humanity in the future.

When I was in my early twenties, I went camping with an organization called The Inchcape Initiative by Raleigh

International. It was part of my assignment for *The Star* newspaper. I enjoy camping. I love nature. We did a lot of outdoor stuff with my dad and brothers. I used to take it for granted. I did not realize how unique it was for an Asian girl to be familiar with surviving the wilds. I was good at managing the rugged outdoors. But I was also good at cooking. This was the other thing I enjoyed. But I hated stereotypes from the time I was young, so I never told anyone that I could cook, especially in the company of boys. I did not want to be the 'designated cook' just because I am a girl. I wanted to do all the dangerous stuff and prove that I was just as good at, or better, than the boys, at activities like pitching tent, setting up the water distiller, starting a fire. So, I hid this gift I had. No one there knew that I could turn canned food and Jell-O into a three-course gourmet meal.

So, one night, when we were out on a mountain forest in Asia and everyone was starving because they did not know what to do with the canned food except to heat it up, I sat there quietly while my two South American mates were struggling just to get the can open. I was one of two girls. The other one was boiling water and potatoes. And then everyone looked at the boiled potatoes without any appetite. That was when I stood up and said, 'Okay, I am going to fix this.' I grabbed the can of meat from the boys. I then asked everyone to wash their camp mugs in the river, wipe it dry, and arrange it on the mat on the campground. Ten mugs in total were arranged in a row. I then took out my secret Eurasian spice, which I had in my bag and which I had spent the last few nights sprinkling into the otherwise bland food, and poured a generous amount into the corned beef and flavoured it. Then I broke bits of cheddar cheese, also from my secret stash, into the mashed potato to make it rich and flavourful. With a generous dollop of spiced corned beef and a topping of cheesy mash, that night the campers ate my deconstructed Shepherd's pie. I even managed to make jelly with the gelatin sheets my friend Tommy

Tanaka's mom had sent him. Due to lack of sugar, the jelly was under sweetened, but no one was complaining. Plates were wiped clean, and people asked for seconds. And then they did what I feared they would do—beg me to cook every night. I remember shouting at Tommy, 'Just because I am a girl doesn't mean I have to cook for all you boys.' Tommy started laughing. He said, 'That's not at all why we want you to cook. You're just a million times better than the rest of us at making something edible. Plus, if you cook, I'll lend you my fancy hiking gloves (Tommy's gloves were the best—practical and cool) and help you carry your bag up really steep slopes.' Now Tommy was a young man who kept his word, and he was incredibly fit and strong—so yes, I reluctantly gave in.

The point I want to make here is that sometimes we do not show parts of ourselves to gratify ourselves. In this case, I did it because I needed to save my campmates from dying of bland food poisoning and to raise the morale of the campers. It is amazing what food can do. You do what you do so others can be inspired, encouraged, fed, and they can rise and simply breathe.

4. My passion spurs my difference. But passion is not something you discover overnight and realize you have. It is something you practice every day.

The spotted zebra does not walk past a mirror one day and realize, 'OMG, I have spots!' You know you are different. You gravitate to different things all your life—the things that make you unique. You keep doing it.

Along the way, you stop being you and gravitating to your passions. Instead, you start reorganizing what you do and reprioritizing your time by a hierarchy set by society. 'Prioritize these things. These are important. The other things you love, they are less important. So, only do them if you have time,' they tell you. What they do not tell you though is what is important and what is not is defined by the value system of a small group of people.

In reality, what is important and what is not, is different from one person to another. We cannot prioritize our time based on what is 'generally deemed important' by society. A spotted zebra spends its time doing what it feels and knows to be important to itself. Otherwise, we end up giving up the things we love—our passion—to live out someone else's priorities and passions.

And the other thing about passion is that it is the most misguided word. We describe someone who quit their stockbroker job to become a yoga teacher as someone who rediscovered their passion. We are programmed by society to think of passion as this singular ambition we had when we were little but strayed away from because of responsibilities and burdens. We think it is that thing we go back to because we suddenly become woke and realize we want to live out our passion—that ambition of our childhood.

Now, here is the reality. When you were a child, you did not know enough to decide what you want to become. So, making any child think of an ambition, a singular job they would work towards getting throughout their middle and high school and university life and stay with throughout their adulthood, is just ridiculous.

You should be allowed to want to do a whole bunch of different things when you are a child, learn a variety of skills you love as a teenager and in university—if you need/want to go to university—and take on jobs that let you use your skills and passion and earn money while doing it. You should be allowed to hold more than one job at a time not just to pay the bills but so you learn new skills and get to make money without getting bored. You should be allowed to change jobs without being judged as an 'irresponsible and disloyal millennial'. Your desire to grow and acquire new skills should be applauded not condemned. That is real ambition and occupation. The power to choose to do the things you love with your waking hours and finding ways to make money doing them.

Let us talk passion. Passion is not one thing that you have. For some people, passion evolves. For some people, like my daughter, it stays. She is twelve. She loves creating things. Every chance she gets, be it with food, soap, candle, fabric, needlework, paint, words—the world is her canvas, and she wants to design, style, and create. It might change when she is older, but since she was in diapers, this has been her passion. And every decision she makes, every action she takes, I can see, it is driven by this singular desire to choose creativity.

For my son, he is still finding his passion. He enjoys building, engineering, strategy gaming. But whatever he does, his passion is to do it with perfection, fine craftsmanship, and finish it well. He is so much like my husband and my dad. Sometimes I think father and son argue because they are so alike. My son has got different passions and is still finding his way through what he totally loves. And that is okay. He is also an awesome pianist and athlete. Outdoor sports come easy to him. Me, my passion is space. From the clothes I wear to the food I eat, I choose something out of this world every time.

What I am trying to say is, as I reflect on everything I have written, I realize we live out our passion not by quitting our jobs and running off to an ashram to meditate. We live out our passion by making daily decisions that are true to what we love and consistent with the things that bring us joy and a sense of achievement.

If your passion is cooking, choose to watch cooking shows. Sign up for cooking classes. Invite friends over who are great foodies and cook for them. Offer to cook something and take the leftover to the office for breakfast. And then perhaps if your intention is to make money from it, when friends and loved ones sample your food, they might be willing to pay to have you cater at their events. Or maybe just bring a dish to a party.

Living out your passion means making decisions and taking actions that are true to your passion every day, at every chance you get. A spotted zebra never misses a chance to choose and live out its passion.

5. I am a computer. I can go obsolete when I do not keep learning.

Now this is an interesting notion I just discovered. And I need you to follow my train of thought as I describe this. As I wrote the different chapters in this book and revisited key moments, I realized there were new lessons that I uncovered. I wondered why I did not see it happen earlier and what had changed. That was when it hit me. We are all computers. Our life experiences, learnings, people we encounter, passing years, and change of environments—these are all software updates. Each time we have a software update, and we revisit a key moment of the past, or experience the same thing again, like reading a book we read at age ten again at age twenty, the breadth and length our life experiences expand. We grow. We advance. But if we stop learning, connecting, and experiencing new things, we become obsolete. We become useless. We have nothing new to impart to the world around us. We need to constantly choose to keep putting ourselves out there, learning and growing.

Recently, I helped my son with his literature homework. He has been reading Shakespeare's *The Merchant of Venice*. I was so happy he was reading it. I read it years back. In fact, I read a lot of Shakespeare's work years back and thought he was brilliant, a talented author, and a man ahead of his time. But this time, when I read it with my son, I was looking at it through the lens of the political and social climate. So much has changed. I had experiences I had never had before. This computer has had a massive software update with new 'social climate' and 'life experience' apps fitted in. And I was able to open and unlock new files I could not before.

Suddenly, I saw Shakespeare's writings differently. Suddenly, I could see the anti-semitism and notion of ancient justice and wisdom through today's lens and realize his writings were so archaic and prejudiced. I started wondering if Shakespeare is the right reading material for kids today. This made me revisit some of Shakespeare's other writings and I realized there was a pattern in how he treated the different social classes. All the jokes and denigration were aimed at the poor, while the rich were made to look intelligent and above reproach. Shakespeare got knocked off his high literary horse and off my list of favourite authors rather quickly. And mind you, before this, he was at the top.

My son was very amused by the turn of events. I embarked on the journey of reading *The Merchant of Venice* with him in excitement, trying to hype up the book, and romanticize Shakespeare as a literary legend, a master playwright. As we went through chapter by chapter, he heard me get frustrated and annoyed at the writing. Daniel was rather pleased. But when he had to study another Shakespeare piece, he said he would do it on his own. I asked him why. He said he was afraid I was going to start a movement to remove Shakespeare from compulsory literature because he was too much of a 'sexist, bigot, class and status conscious kept-man who was a misogynist'. 'Sometimes, mom, it's just a book you have to read to get through the exams. I know you are not okay with that. But I am.' And so, out of love and respect for my son, once again I left it and walked away.

6. My intelligence is subjective. My kindness is universal.

As a teenager, I spent six months in the jungles of Malaysia with a group of tribal people in pursuit of religious enlightenment. I had read about how they had an encounter with God and experienced miracles, and I wanted to find out more. All the physics and modern technology I knew were useless here. What was useful was learning which leaves I could touch and eat fresh, which should be cooked and eaten, and which I should steer clear of. How and where to look out for pythons. What to do when I see one. How to use natural products found in the rainforest to heal cuts and bruises. And most importantly, a few words in the tribal language to communicate my basic needs—food, hungry, toilet, danger, help.

When I was a journalist, the kind of intelligence that was needed was the ability to research a topic completely foreign to me, knowing how to ask the right questions, understanding what the right question for each story would be, who I should interview for this story, and where and how I was going to find this person or people.

In the Google era, it is no longer about what and how much I know. It is about identifying what I need to know and finding the right tools and keywords to access the information I need.

Intelligence is a spectrum. It takes different forms in different places, and under different circumstances. The smartest person in one environment may not be the smartest in every environment. In fact, despite being an A student during my teenage years, I felt like a noob in the jungle with people younger than me married and raising families as they protected and provided for their homes. I felt very humbled and at times incredibly useless because all my education meant nothing there. There was simply no room for intellectual snobbery.

But whether it is in a royal palace in London or in a humble hut in rural India, I have found that kindness is universal. Everyone understands it. And the love and hospitality you get when you extend kindness and mercy to people transcends education and cultural differences. Kindness trumps intellect anytime and should be turned into a currency.

7. It is okay to be inspired by people who do not match my standards of morality.

I love Elon Musk. I honestly believe he is paving the foundation for a better future for my children. I have been a fan long before he became the official world's richest man. I am also a big fan of Tony Stark, the Iron Man. See the similarity. It is not the shiny suits. I love robots and space. I have been following Elon Musk since his PayPal days. I have read all the books about him and made a learned choice to follow him and believe in the things he is pursuing—e-commerce, clean energy, better transportation systems, space travel. I am an even bigger fan of his mom, Maye. She is a remarkable woman who has broken many stereotypes. She is 78 and living her best life. She has raised three amazing children. And I am a big Michelle Obama fangirl—she is so smart, elegant, and inspiring.

I also speak on gender equality and women empowerment. I am often asked, how can you like Elon? He stands for everything you do not. It always surprises me because people think my fascination with someone must be based on their moral values and that I can only get behind people who share my values. I do share an aspect of what he champions—innovation and pushing humanity into a whole new era of progress. It excites me and fills me with hope that humanity is not plateauing as a civilization. And because of that, there will be great advancements made to support my children's generation. It does not mean I agree with his personal life and the reports on mistreatment of women in the organizations he owns. We often mix up the two and make ourselves the guardians of the world's morality. But I try not to judge people's behaviour unless they are consciously attacking and threatening human rights. I refuse to cast a stone.

Do not let a person's flaws blind you to their inspiration. Otherwise, there is no one that matters that the spotted zebra can be inspired by. Because as long as they are public figures, they are under scrutiny, and their flaws get magnified for all to see.

8. I need to make room for opinions and actions I do not agree with.

This was the most important lesson I learned. And the most difficult one to put to practice. To sit in a room full of opinions that go against your values and allow it to continue is the highest sign of maturity. To agree that this opinion that you are against should be shared with the public so they can decide for themselves if it is good or bad, right or wrong—that requires a new level of enlightenment. But a spotted zebra knows that information and opinions are just that—knowledge. Knowledge is not the same as wisdom. Wisdom is taking knowledge, digesting it, and then applying it with understanding. And everyone has a right to be exposed to diverse knowledge and be allowed to choose what they want to digest, apply, and turn into their wisdom.

I have also learned that opposing arguments can often be two sides of the same coin. You are both looking at an identical thing through different lenses. And only through seeing both sides of an argument can you arrive at a full story. Society says take the right side. A spotted zebra allows for both sides to be presented to uncover the 'full side' and arrive at the complete truth.

9. The need to be popular puts the choices of our lives in the hands of the masses.

I mentioned this in a previous chapter. But as I reflected on this through the lens of a spotted zebra, it became much clearer. Jay Shetty asked a friend who had bought a brand new BWM but could barely afford the down payment the reason for doing that. He said, 'Driving a car like this makes me look good in the eyes of others.' Imagine making a hefty down payment so you look good in the eyes of complete strangers. If we removed the need to be popular through the lens of someone else, what choices would you make differently? How different would your life be? I drive a Tesla. My husband made the decision to buy the car. I asked him why. It is a ridiculously expensive car in Singapore. He laughed and said, 'I am buying it because you believe in it. It will make you happy. And when you are happy, I will be happy.' He was so right. I know people will judge me and call it a waste of money. But that car brought so much joy to my heart. I knew that I was investing in a brand and a technology I fully believed in. And for my husband, from a design, engineering, and technology perspective, it is the best car he has driven. So, we both won. We bought the car for ourselves. And the joy that we got from it was priceless. Make choices for yourself, not to feed and fan the opinions of others about you.

10. I need to keep making connections. The connections do not all have to be forever. They just need to keep happening.

I wrote in a previous chapter on the power of making new connections. How this was the number one secret ingredient to a long life. While the spotted zebra is different from the others in its community, it is not a lone zebra. It is connected and makes connections as it moves along. Its uniqueness piques the curiosity of other zebras and draws them to it. Your uniqueness will draw people to you. You could shut them out or avoid them. Or keep connecting with them. I personally find this a struggle. I find it easier to stand on stage and speak to tens of thousands than to sit and talk to a smaller group of people. I do not do small talk well.

But there is also something strange about this spotted zebra. Leave me sitting alone for ten minutes and a total stranger will come by and—to my absolute horror—start sharing intimate details about his/her entire life. My husband usually stands behind a pole, hides and spies on the action, eaves dropping, completely amused. He has seen this happen from the day we started dating. People love to offload their life stories on me. I used to find it overwhelming till I heard about how connecting has the power to extend your life. So, now I welcome people when they start talking to me. I listen actively. And I have started saying hello to everyone of all ages in the parking lot, in the lift, from all walks of lives—old folks, young folks, babies, kids, teenagers. They usually want to run away screaming. Just the other day, I had a conversation with two of the neighbour's parrots, perched on their gate. I know it sounds crazy, but the birds engaged me first. One could only sing, and it sang rather sweetly. The other, a rather gigantic fowl, the length of my elbow, spoke in a low pitch pirate's parrot voice. And it said the strangest things like, 'Go back', 'Out of sight, out of mind', 'Arrr boom boom.' After a five-minute conversation, I continued my walk to the neighbourhood cold storage with one parrot whistling and the other yelling 'Come back' in the background.

I may never see the birds again. But the point is that I do not have to build deep connections. But a spotted zebra must always stay connected.

11. My voice matters. I do not have to be loud, aggressive, or charismatic to be heard.

One of my favourite Rumi quote is, 'Raise your words, not your voice. It is rain that grows flowers, not thunder.' My kids quote that to me when I yell at them for messing up the house. But it is true of everything in life. While spotted zebras need to own their uniqueness, they do not have to shout their uniqueness out at people. They simply have to be and let their uniqueness shine, and it will draw its own crowd.

When I was working in the big ad agencies, the temptation as a female leader was to borrow the qualities of the male leaders. To speak in a loud, assertive manner. To let logic trump mercy and empathy in the decisions I made. To look tough and not be too feminine. But I am naturally feminine—well, cool feminine, I love my leather, studs, and denim and the whole rocker chic look. And I prefer to lead with empathy and kindness versus play the logic card. And I hate yelling. I have a naturally loud voice because I sing and take vocal lessons to help me project. But I hate being shouted at and do not enjoy shouting at my team to intimidate them. So, I had to choose to lead not as another successful leader but as the unique leader that I am. Fortunately, we live in a time today where you can see humble, soft-spoken people hold positions of leadership.

Rosa Parks, who in 1955 refused to give her seat up for white men, was a great example of a soft-spoken woman who did something brave quietly. In the introduction of her book *Quiet: The Power of Introverts in a World That Can't Stop Talking*, Susan Cain states[30], 'I had always imagined Rosa Parks as a stately woman with a bold temperament, someone who could easily stand up to a busload of glowering passengers. But when she died in 2005 at the age of ninety-two, the flood of obituaries recalled her as soft-spoken, sweet, and small in stature. They said that she was 'timid and shy' but had 'the courage of a lion'. They were full of phrases like 'radical humility' and 'quiet fortitude'.

The former Yahoo! CEO may be well-known, but Marissa Mayer still believes in quiet leadership and has admitted that 'I'm just geeky and shy and I like to code.'[31] And, of course, I have to

---

[30] Susan Cain, *Quiet: The Power of Introverts in a World That Can't Stop Talking* (Penguin Random House, 2013).

[31] Kamran Ali, 'Introverts can be great leaders', *Medium*, 2021, https://kamranali09. medium.com/introverts-can-be-great-leaders-88dc8bc08610.

mention Elon Musk who has Asperger's and is obviously awkward when he gives speeches. Musk has been open about how he went from an 'introverted engineer' to the next Steve Jobs[32].

I have a very charismatic son and a very reserved (not to be mistaken for timid) daughter. They are so different in personality. But leaders come in unique shapes and forms. The societal notion that you must be charismatic and an extrovert who is loud and gregarious to lead has long been a busted myth. The best way you can be a spotted zebra and lead is by identifying your uniqueness and leading with your own authentic voice.

And with that, the last chapter of this book comes to an end, by encouraging all you spotted zebras out there to wear your spots with pride.

---

[32] Caroline Castrillon, 'How Introverts Can Thrive As Entrepreneurs', *Forbes*, 2019, https://www.forbes.com/sites/carolinecastrillon/2019/01/23/how-introverts-can-thrive-as-entrepreneurs/?sh=35af09b75cac.

Acknowledgements

This book would not have been possible if I was not alive today. I believe there is a power greater than us, that is responsible for the creation of all things, that makes my heart sing every day and breathes life into my body. I want to thank this greater power, my Maker—the one who blessed me with a life of purpose and a beautiful family.

Then there's my family. Colin, my husband who adores me, my two beautiful teenage kids, Daniel and Sarah who have a special way to keep me grounded, and our two fur babies, Chewbarka and Moose who have a magical way of putting me on a pedestal, especially when I have treats in hand. You gave your time, love and support to me and believed I could do anything. Thank you for being my anchor and my light house, always keeping me on track and leading me to safe harbour.

Here's a shout out to all the spotted zebras who've inspired me through history—an endless list—I dare not mention names lest I forget one and have to live with the guilt of it once this book is published.

I want to thank all the people who influenced my life knowingly, unknowingly and historically. You continue to teach me. And I continue to grow and learn. Big thank you to my mum and my late dad, Naomi and Benny, Gene Roddenberry, the creator of Star Trek who sparked my imagination and continues to spur my love for theoretical physics, the late David Ogilvy whose books and philosophy taught me the art of selling by uncovering the human need, Optimus Prime, the noble leader of the autobots—though you're fictional, you made me reevaluate some of my life's values in a big way and rethink what it means to be human, organic and created. And finally to all my imaginary friends—thank you for keeping my imagination alive and thriving.

To all of you who consider yourselves my friends, thanks for accepting me despite the strangeness. Though I am pretty sure that's the real reason why we are friends! Kylee Vowles, a shout out to you my business partner who puts up with my madness 5 days a week and sometimes, even more.

And to all of you who bought this book whether to support me, or simply because the title grabbed your attention, or because you identify as a spotted zebra—whatever the reason, I am grateful. I hope you get something awesome out of it.